AF517908

ISSUES in JOURNALISM and MASS COMMUNICATION

D.K. GUPTA

RAJAT PUBLICATIONS
NEW DELHI - 110 002 (INDIA)

RAJAT PUBLICATIONS
4675/21, Ansari Road, Daryaganj
New Delhi- 110 002 (India)
Phones : 23267924, 22507277
E-mail: rajat_publication@yahoo.com

Issues in Journalism and Mass Communication

© *Author*

Edition 2025

ISBN 978-81-7880-227-9

[All rights reserved. No part of this publication may be reproduced, stored in a retrieval system or transmitted, in any form or by any means, mechanical, photocopying, recording or otherwise, without prior written permission of the publisher].

PRINTED IN INDIA

Published by Mrs. Seema Wasan for Rajat Publications, New Delhi and Printed atTarun Offset Press, Delhi.

Preface

Journalism is a profession related with the dissemination of news and views and as such journalists should work out of motivation and idealism for the truth, and journalism ethics should be about aspirations and goals rather than minimum standards. The difficulty is that ethical journalists first need to be moral journalists; and to be moral journalists they must first believe in some kind of overriding of conduct and belief. Professional ethics should make all aware of the need for aspirations and principles rather than rules.

Journalism ethics and standards include principles of ethics and of good practice to address the specific challenges faced by professional journalists. These principles are most widely known to journalists as their professional code of ethics of the canons of journalism. By emphasising the importance of personal integrity and collective concern for serving the public's right to know the result will be a cohort of journalists who will actively seek the best possible journalism. A clear and unequivocal emphasis on duty, responsibility and the vital role played by the media in a democratic society should make it abundantly clear to all journalists what sort of behaviour is expected from them.

This book analyses various principles and issues of modern journalism. It is designed for students and professionals of journalism and mass communication.

Editor

Contents

1

Mass Media Development

The history of modern media begins with the printed book—certainly a kind of revolution, yet initially only a technical device for reproducing a range of texts the same as, or similar to, what was already being extensively copied by hand. Only gradually does printing lead to a change in content—more secular, practical and popular works, as well as political and religious pamphlets and tracts—which played a part in the transformation of the medieval world.

At an early date, laws and proclamations were also printed by royal and other authorities. Thus, there occurred a revolution of society in which printing played an inseparable part. The antecedents of the book lie in classical times when there were numerous established authors and when works of many kinds, both fictional and nonfictional, were copied and circulated for reading or verbal transmission. In the west, at least, the culture of the book largely disappeared after the end of the Roman Empire until revived by monastic activities, although some key texts were preserved for reasons of learning or religion.

In the early medieval period, the book was not regarded primarily as a means of communication. Rather it was a store or repository of wisdom and especially of sacred writings and religious texts that had to be kept in uncorrupted form. Around the central core of religious and philosophical texts there accumulated also works of science and practical information. The main material form of the book at this time was of bound volumes of separate pages within strong covers, which is known as the codex, reflecting the requirements for safe storage and reading aloud from a lectern plus the demands of travel and transportation.

Books were meant both to last and to be disseminated within limited circles. The modern book is a direct descendant of this model, and similar uses are embedded within it. The alternative form of rolls of paper or parchment was discontinued, especially when the printing press replaced writing by hand and required the pressing of flat sheets. This ensured the triumph of the medieval manuscript book format, even when miniaturised. Another important element of continuity between writing and printing is the library, a store or collection of books. This remained similar in concept and physical arrangement, at least until the advent of digital libraries.

It also reflected and confirmed the idea of a book as a record or permanent work of reference. The character of the library did not change much with printing, although printing stimulated the acquisition of private libraries. The later development of the library has given it some claim to be considered not only as a medium but even as a mass medium. It is certainly often organised as a means of public information and was envisaged from the mid nineteenth century onwards as an important tool of mass enlightenment. The successful application of print technology to the reproduction of texts in place of handwriting, about the mid fifteenth century, was only the first step in the emergence of a 'media institution'.

Printing gradually became a new craft and a significant branch of commerce. Printers were later transformed from tradespeople into publishers, and the two functions gradually became distinct. Equally important was the emergence of the idea and role of the 'author' since earlier manuscript texts were not typically authored by living individuals. A natural further development was the role of professional author, as early as the late sixteenth century, typically supported by wealthy patrons. Each of these developments reflects the emergence of a market and the transformation of the book into a commodity. Although print runs were small by modern standards, cumulative sales over time could be large.

The later history of the book is one of steady expansion in volume and range of content and also of struggle for freedom of the press and the rights of authors. Nearly everywhere from the early sixteenth century onwards, government and church authorities applied advance censorship to printed matter, even if not with the effectiveness of a modern totalitarian state. The most famous early and eloquent claim for freedom from government licensing was made by the English poet John Milton in a tract published in 1644 (Areopagitica). Freedom of the press went hand in hand with democratic political freedoms and the former was only achieved where democracy triumphed.

NEWSPAPER

It was almost 200 years after the invention of printing before what we now recognise as a prototypical newspaper could be distinguished from the handbills, pamphlets and newsletters of the late sixteenth and early seventeenth centuries. Its chief precursor seems, in fact, to have been the letter rather than the book—newsletters circulating through the rudimentary postal service, concerned especially with transmitting news of events relevant to international trade and commerce. It was thus an extension into the public sphere of an activity that had long taken place for governmental, diplomatic or commercial purposes. The early newspaper was marked by its regular appearance, commercial basis (openly for sale), public character and multiple purpose. Thus, it was used for information, record, advertising, diversion and gossip.

The seventeenth-century commercial newspaper was not identified with any single source but was a compilation made by a printer-publisher. The official variety showed some of the same characteristics but was also a voice of authority and an instrument of state. The commercial newspaper was the form which has given most shape to the newspaper institution, and its development can be seen in retrospect as a major turning point in communication history—offering first of all a service to its anonymous readers rather than an instrument to propagandists or authorities. In a sense the newspaper was more of an innovation than the printed book—the invention of a new literary, social and cultural form—even if it might not have been so perceived at the time.

Its distinctiveness, compared with other forms of cultural communication, lies in its orientation to the individual reader and to reality, its utility and disposability, and its secularity and suitability for the needs of a new class: town-based business and professional people. Its novelty consisted not in its technology or manner of distribution, but in its functions for a distinct class in a changing and more liberal social-political climate. The later history of the newspaper can be told either as a series of struggles, advances and reverses in the cause of liberty or as a more continuous history of economic and technological progress.

The most important phases in press history that enter into the modern definition of the newspaper are described in the following paragraphs. While separate national histories differ too much to tell a single story, the elements mentioned, often intermingling and interacting, have all played a part in the development of the press institution. From its early days, the newspaper was an actual or a potential adversary of established power, especially in its own self-perception. Potent images in press history refer to violence done to printers, editors and journalists.

The struggle for freedom to publish, often within a broader movement for freedom, democracy and citizen rights, is emphasised. The part played by underground presses under foreign occupation or dictatorial rule has also been celebrated. Established authority has often confirmed this self-perception of the press by finding it irritating and inconvenient. However, early newspapers did not generally seek to offend authorities and were sometimes produced on their behalf. Then, as now, the newspaper was likely to identify most with its intended readers. There has been a steady progression towards more press freedom, despite major setbacks from time to time. This progress has sometimes taken the form of greater sophistication in the means of control applied to the press.

Legal restraint replaced violence, then fiscal burdens were imposed. Now institutionalisation of the press within a market system serves as a form of control, and the modern newspaper, as a large business enterprise, is vulnerable to more kinds of pressure or intervention than its simpler forerunners were. The newspaper did not really become a true 'mass' medium until the twentieth century, in the sense of directly reaching a majority of the population on a regular basis, and there are still quite large intercountry differences in the extent of newspaper reading. It has been customary and it is still useful to distinguish between certain types or genres of newspaper, although there is no single typology to suit all epochs and countries.

One common early form of the newspaper was the party-political paper dedicated to the task of activation, information and organisation. The party newspaper has lost ground to commercial press forms, both as an idea and as a viable business enterprise. The idea of a party press, even so, still has its place as a component in democratic politics. Where it does survive in Europe, it is typically independent from the state, professionally produced, serious and opinion-forming in purpose. Its uniqueness lies in the attachment of its readers by way of shared party allegiance, its sectionalism and its mobilising function for party objectives. Examples include the 'vanguard press' of the Russian revolutionary movement, the party-political newspapers of several Scandinavian countries and the official party press of former communist regimes.

The late-nineteenth-century bourgeois newspaper was a high point in press history and contributed much to the modern understanding of what a newspaper is or should be. The 'high-bourgeois' phase of press history, from about 1850 to the turn of the century, was the product of several events and circumstances. These included: the triumph of liberalism and the absence or ending of direct censorship or fiscal constraint; the forging of a business-professional establishment; plus many social and technological changes favouring the rise of a national or regional press of high information quality. The new prestige or 'elite' press was independent from the state and from vested interests and often recognised as a major institution of political and social life.

It tended to show a highly developed sense of social and ethical responsibility and it fostered the rise of a journalistic profession dedicated to the objective reporting of events. Many countries still have one or more newspapers that try to maintain this tradition. Current expectations about what is a 'quality' newspaper still reflect the professional ideals of the prestige press and provide the basis for criticisms of newspapers which deviate from the ideal by being either too partisan or too 'sensational'.

The last main type of newspaper has been with us for a century or so without much change of essential character. This is the truly 'mass' newspaper that was created for sale to the urban industrial masses and designed to be read by almost everyone. It was a fundamentally commercial enterprise (rather than a political or professional project) and was made possible by advances in technologies of scale, concentrations of population, the spread of literacy, low cost to the reader and large amounts of advertising revenue. In general, the popular press has always specialised in 'human interest' stories, in dramatic and sensational styles of reporting and presentation, in the coverage of crime, disasters, crises, scandals, war and celebrities.

Although not primarily interested in politics, it has often played a political role at key moments in national societies. Because of its typical format, the term 'tabloid' has been widely applied to this type of newspaper and its contents, as in the phrase 'tabloidisation'. This means a process of becoming more sensational, trivial and irresponsible. In many countries, the most important newspaper sectors have been and remain the local and regional press. The forms are too varied to be described as a single type. They can be serious or popular, daily or weekly, urban or rural, with large as well as small circulations.

The main features they have in common are: a set of news values relevant to a local readership; a typically consensual and bipartisan approach (although there are exceptions) ; a dependence on support from local advertisers. The printing press gave rise to other forms of publication than book and newspaper. These include plays, songs, tracts, serial stories, poems, pamphlets, comics, reports, prospectuses, maps, posters, music, handbills, wall newspapers and much more.

The single most significant is probably the periodical (weekly or monthly) magazine that appeared in great diversity and with wide circulations from the early eighteenth century onwards. Initially aimed at the domestic and cultural interests of the gentry, it eventually developed into a mass market of high commercial value and enormous breadth of coverage. The periodical magazine still belongs largely to the domestic and personal sphere and supports a wide range of interests, activities and markets.

In the early twentieth century it was more like a mass medium than it is today, and its diffuseness and uncertain impact have led to a general neglect by communication research. These comments apply to the commercial periodical. In many countries there has been and remains a significant opinion-forming or political periodical press, often with an influence beyond its circulation size. At key moments in some societies particular magazines have played important social, cultural or political roles. In conditions of political oppression or commercial domination the 'alternative' periodical has often been an essential instrument of resistance and expression for minority movements.

Film

Film began at the end of the nineteenth century as a

technological novelty, but what it offered was scarcely new in content or function. It transferred to a new means of presentation and distribution an older tradition of entertainment, offering stories, spectacles, music, drama, humour and technical tricks for popular consumption. It was also almost instantly a true mass medium in the sense that it quite quickly reached a very large proportion of populations, even in rural areas. As a mass medium, film was partly a response to the 'invention' of leisure—time out of work—and an answer to the demand for affordable and (usually) respectable ways of enjoying free time for the whole family. Thus it provided for the working class some of the cultural benefits already enjoyed by their social 'betters'. To judge from its phenomenal growth, the latent demand met by film was enormous.

Of the main formative elements named above, it would not be the technology or the social climate but the needs met by the film for individuals that mattered most. The characterisation of the film as 'show business' in a new form for an expanded market is not the whole story. There have been three other significant strands in film history. First, the use of film for propaganda is noteworthy, especially when applied to national or societal purposes, based on its great reach, supposed realism, emotional impact and popularity. The two other strands in film history were the emergence of several schools of film art and the rise of the social documentary film movement. These were different from the mainstream in having either a minority appeal or a strong element of realism (or both).

Both have a link, partly fortuitous, with film as propaganda in that both tended to develop at times of social crisis. There continue to be thinly concealed ideological and implicitly propagandist elements in many popular entertainment films, even in politically 'free' societies. This reflects a mixture of forces: deliberate attempts at social control; unthinking adoption of populist or conservative values; various marketing and PR infiltrations into entertainment; and the pursuit of mass appeal. Despite the dominance of the entertainment function in film history, films have often displayed didactic propagandistic tendencies.

Film is certainly more vulnerable than other media to outside interference and may be more subject to conformist pressures because so much capital is at risk. It is a reflection of this situation that in the aftermath of the 9/11 attack on the Twin Towers, US government leaders sought a meeting with leaders of the film industry to discuss ways in which film could make a contribution to the newly announced 'war on terror'. Three turning points in film history have been the 'Americanisation' of the film industry and film culture in the years after the First World War, the coming of television and the separation of film from the cinema.

The relative decline of nascent, but flourishing, European film industries at that time probably contributed to a homogenisation of film culture and a convergence of ideas about the definition of film as a medium. Television took away a large part of the film-viewing public, especially the general family audience, leaving a much smaller and younger film audience. It also took away or diverted the social documentary stream of film development and gave it a more congenial home in television. However, it did not do the same for the art film or for film aesthetics, although the art film may have benefited from the 'demassification' and greater specialisation of the film/cinema medium.

For the first two generations of filmgoers, the film experience was inseparable from having an evening out, usually with friends and usually in venues that were far grander than the home. In addition, the darkened cinema offered a mixture of privacy and sociability that gave another dimension to the experience. Just as with television later, 'going to the pictures' was as important as seeing any particular film.

The 'separation of film and cinema' refers to the many ways in which films can be seen, after initial showing in a film theatre. These include television broadcasting, cable transmission, videotape and DVD sale or hire, satellite TV and now broadband Internet. These developments have several potential consequences. They make film less typically a public experience and more a private one. They reduce the initial 'impact' of mass exposure to a given film. They shift control of selection in the direction of the audience and allow new patterns of repeat viewing and collection. They make it possible to serve many specialist markets and easier to cater for the demand for violent, horrific or pornographic content.

Despite the liberation entailed in becoming a less 'mass' medium, the film has not been able to claim full rights to political and artistic self-expression, and most countries retain an apparatus of licensing, censorship and powers of control. Although the cinema has been subordinated to television in many ways, it has also become more integrated with other media, especially book publishing, popular music and television itself. It has acquired a greater centrality, despite the reduction of its immediate audience, as a showcase for other media and as a cultural source, out of which come books, strip cartoons, songs, and television 'stars' and series. Thus, film is as much as ever a mass culture creator. Even the loss of the cinema audience has been more than compensated by a new domestic film audience reached by television, video recordings, cable and satellite channels.

Broadcasting

Radio and television have, respectively, an eighty-plus- and a fifty-plus-year history as mass media, and both grew out of preexisting technologies—telephone, telegraph, moving and still photography, and sound recording. Despite their obvious differences of content and use, radio and television can be treated together in terms of their history. Radio seems to have been a technology looking for a use, rather than a response to a demand for a new kind of service or content, and much the same is true of television.

According to Williams, 'Unlike all previous communications technologies, radio and television were systems primarily designed for transmission and reception as abstract processes, with little or no definition of preceding content. ' Both came to borrow from existing media, and most of the popular content forms of both are derivative from film, music, stories, news and sport.

A distinctive feature of radio and television has been their high degree of regulation, control or licensing by public authority—initially out of technical necessity, later from a mixture of democratic choice, state self-interest, economic convenience and sheer institutional custom. A second and related feature of radio and television media has been their centre—periphery pattern of distribution and the association of national television with political life and the power centres of society, as it became established as both popular and politically important. Despite, or perhaps because cf, this closeness to power, radio and television have hardly anywhere acquired, as of right, the same freedom that the press enjoys, to express views and act with political independence.

Television has been continuously evolving, and it would be risky to try to summarise its features in terms of communicative purposes and effects. Initially the main genre innovation of television stemmed from its capacity to transmit many pictures and sound live and thus act as a 'window on the world' in real time. Even studio productions were live broadcasts before the days of efficient video recording. This capacity of simultaneity has been retained for some kinds of content, including sporting events, some newscasting, and certain kinds of entertainment show.

Most TV content is not live, although it often aims to create an illusion of ongoing reality. A second important feature of television is the sense of intimacy and personal involvement that it seems able to cultivate between the spectator and presenter or the actors and participants on screen. The status of television as the most 'massive' of the media in terms of reach, time spent and popularity has barely changed over thirty years and it adds all the time to its global audience. Even so, there are significant intercountry differences in its dominance of free time. Despite the fact that television has been largely denied an autonomous political role and is primarily considered a medium of entertainment, it plays a vital role in modern politics.

It is considered to be the main source of news and information for most people and the main channel of communication between politicians and citizens, especially at election times. In this informally allocated role of public informer, television has generally remained credible and trusted. Another role is that of educator—for children at school and adults at home. It is also the largest single channel of advertising in nearly all countries, and this has helped to confirm its mass entertainment functions. So far, many predictions that mass television would fragment into many different channels, along the model of the magazine, have only been partially realised, although the process is likely to accelerate as digitalisation proceeds.

Nevertheless one enduring feature of the appeal of television seems to lie in the very fact that it is a medium that brings people together to share the same experiences in an otherwise fragmented and individuated society and not only in the circle of the family. Radio notably refused to die in the face of the rise of television and it has prospered on the basis of several distinctive features. Competition with television led to a degree of deliberate differentiation. After a pirate phase, radio shed its burden of being a highly regulated national 'voice' and became more free to experiment and to express new, minority and even deviant sounds in voice and music. As a medium it has much more channel capacity and therefore much more and more diverse access.

It is much cheaper and more flexible in production than television and also cheap and flexible in use for its audience. There are no longer limitations on the place where radio can be listened to or the time of reception, since listening can be combined with other routine activities. It has possibilities for interaction with its audience by way of the telephone and can accommodate many different genres. In fact radio has flourished since the coming of television, even if it can no longer claim the mass audience of its glory days in the 1940s.

Music

Relatively little attention has been given to music as a mass medium in theory and research, perhaps because the implications for society have never been clear, nor have there been sharp discontinuities in the possibilities offered by successive technologies of recording and reproduction/ transmission. Recorded and replayed music has not even

enjoyed a convenient label to describe its numerous media manifestations, although the generic term 'phonogram' has been suggested to cover music accessed via record players, tape players, compact disc players, VCRs (video cassette recorders), broadcasting and cable, etc. The recording and replaying of music began around 1880 and records werequite rapidly diffused, on the basis of the wide appeal of popular songs and melodies. Their popularity and diffusion were closely related to the already established place of the piano (and other instruments) in the home.

Much radio content since the early days has consisted of music, even more so since the rise of television. While there may have been a gradual tendency for the 'phonogram' to replace private music-making, there has never been a large gap between mass mediated music and personal and direct audience enjoyment of musical performance (concerts, choirs, bands, dances, etc.). The phonogram makes music of all kinds more accessible at all times in more places to more people, but it is hard to discern a fundamental discontinuity in the general character of popular musical experience, despite changes of genre and fashion. Even so, there have been big changes in the broad character of the phonogram since its beginnings. The first change was the addition of radio broadcast music to phonogram records, which greatly increased the range and amount of music available and extended it to many more people than had access to gramophones or jukeboxes.

The transition of radio from a family to an individual medium in the post-war 'transistor' revolution was a second major change, which opened up a relatively new market of young people for what became a burgeoning record industry. The growth of music downloading and sharing via the Internet has added to the distribution traffic and seriously challenged the power of music rights holders.

While the cultural significance of music has received sporadic attention, its relationship to social and political events has been recognised and occasionally celebrated or feared. Since the rise of the youth-based industry in the 1960s, mass-mediated popular music has been linked to youthful idealism and political concern, to supposed degeneration and hedonism, to drug-taking, violence and antisocial attitudes. Music has also played a part in various nationalist independence movements (e. g. Ireland and Estonia).

While the content of music has never been easy to regulate, its distribution has predominantly been in the hands of established institutions, and its perceived deviant tendencies have been subject to some sanctions. Aside from this, most popular music has continued to express and respond to rather enduring conventional values and personal needs.

New and Traditional Media

The expression 'new media' has been in use since the 1960s and has had to encompass an expanding and diversifying set of applied communication technologies. As far as the essential features of 'new media' are concerned, the main ones seem to be: their interconnectedness; their accessibility to individual users as senders and/or receivers; their interactivity; their multiplicity of use and open-ended character; and their ubiquity and 'delocatedness'. The ongoing 'communications revolution' is seen by some as a revolt against mass communication, an idea that has a long history in critical theory. The two main driving forces of change are: satellite communication and the harnessing of the computer.

The key to the immense power of the computer as a communication machine lies in the process of digitalisation that allows information of all kinds in all formats to be carried with the same efficiency and also intermingled. In principle there is no longer any need for the various different media that have been described, since all could be subsumed in the same computerised communication network and reception centre. In practice there is no sign of this happening. Alongside computer-based technologies there are other innovations that have in some degree changed some aspects of mass communication.

New means of transmission by cable, satellite and radio have immensely increased the capacity to transmit. New means of storage and retrieval, including the personal video recorder, CD-ROM, compact disc, DVD, etc., have also expanded the range of possibilities, and even the remote control device has played a part. While not directly supporting mass communication, the many new possibilities for private 'media-making' have expanded the world of media and forged bridges between public and private communication and between the spheres of professional and amateur.

Finally, we should note the new kinds of 'quasi-media' including computer games and virtual reality devices that overlap with the media in their culture and in the satisfactions of use. The implications of all this for mass media are still far from clear, although it is certain that the 'traditional' media have also benefited greatly from new media innovations as well as acquiring new competitors. Secondly, we can already conclude that the communications revolution has generally shifted the 'balance of power' from the media to the audience, in so far as there are more options to choose from and more active uses of media available. Traditional mass communication was essentially one-directional, while the new forms of communication are essentially interactive.

Mass communication has in several respects become less massive and less centralised. Beyond that, it is useful to distinguish between the implications of enhanced transmission and the emergence of any new medium as such. In respect of transmission, the main changes so far have been in the capacity of the networks and the increased volume of traffic, at lower costs all round. Amongst this, one of the most important facts is the emergence of a somewhat new kind of interpersonal network based on the mobile phone, which is still in search of its uses. As far as the traditional media are concerned, there have not yet been major shifts in the type of content or in the range of uses.

Media and Society

Relations between media and society have a material, a political and a normative or social-cultural dimension. Central to the political dimension is the question of freedom and control. The main normative issue concerns how media ought to use the freedom they have. Near-total freedom was claimed and eventually gained for the book, for a mixture of reasons, in which the claims of politics, religion, science and art all played some part. This situation remains unchallenged in free societies, although the book has lost some of its once subversive potential as a result of its relative marginalisation. The influence of books remains considerable, but has to a large extent to be mediated through other more popular media or other institutions (education, politics, etc.).

The newspaper press bases its historical claim to freedom of operation much more directly on its political functions of expressing opinion and circulating political and economic information. But the newspaper is also a significant business enterprise for which freedom to produce and supply its primary product (information) is a necessary condition of successful operation in the marketplace. Broadcast television and radio are still generally licensed and have limited political freedom in practice, partly because of their privileged access to scarce spectrum space (despite the proclaimed 'end of scarcity') and partly because of their believed impact and power to persuade.

But they are also often expected to use their informative capacity to support the democratic process and serve the public good in other ways. Even so, the current trend is for market forces to have a greater influence on the conduct of broadcasting than either political control or voluntary social responsibility. The various new media, using cable, satellite or telecommunications networks for distribution, still await clear definitions of their appropriate degree of political freedom. The key new medium in this respect is the Internet.

Freedom from control may be claimed on the grounds of privacy or the fact that these are not media of indiscriminate mass distribution but are directed to specific users. They are so-called 'common carriers' that generally escape control over their content. They also increasingly share the same communicative tasks as media with established editorial autonomy. The question remains in dispute for a number of reasons, among them the need for regulation for technical reasons or to prevent abuse of monopoly power. The intermedia differences relating to political control follow a general pattern.

In practice this means that the nearer any medium gets to operating as a mass medium, the more it can expect the attentions of governments, since it affects the exercise of power. In general, activities in the sphere of fiction, fantasy or entertainment are more likely to escape attention than are activities that touch directly on the ongoing reality of events and circumstances. Virtually all media of public communication have a radical potential, in the sense of being potentially subversive of reigning systems of social control. They can provide access for new voices and perspectives on the existing order; new forms of organisation and protest are made available for the subordinate or disenchanted.

2

World Wide Web in Journalism

The World Wide Web ("WWW" or simply the "Web") is a global, read-write information space. Text documents, images, multimedia and many other items of information, referred to as resources, are identified by short, unique, global identifiers called Uniform Resource Identifiers (URIs) so that each can be found, accessed and cross-referenced in the simplest possible way. The term is often mistakenly used as a synonym for the Internet itself, but the Web is actually something that is available over the Internet, just like e-mail and many other Internet services. The World Wide Web is the combination of four basic ideas:

- Hypertext, that is the ability, in a computer environment, to move from one part of a document to another or from one document to another through internal connections among these documents (called " hyperlinks");
- Resource Identifiers, that is the ability, on a computer network, to locate a particular resource (computer file, document or other resource) on the network through a unique identifier;
- The Client-server model of computing, in which client software or a client computer makes requests of server

software or a server computer that provides the client with resources or services, such as data or files; and

– Markup language, in which characters or codes embedded in text indicate structure, semantic meaning or advice on presentation.

On the World Wide Web, a client program called a web browser retrieves information resources, such as web pages and other computer files, from web servers using their URLs and displays them, typically on a computer monitor. One can then follow hyperlinks in each page to other resources on the World Wide Web whose location is provided by these hyperlinks. It is also possible, for example by filling in and submitting web forms, to post information back to a server to interact with it. The act of following hyperlinks is often called "browsing" or "surfing" the Web.

Web pages are often arranged in collections of related material called "websites." The phrase "surfing the Internet" was first popularised in print by Jean Armour Polly, a librarian, in an article called Surfing the INTERNET, published in the Wilson Library Bulletin in June, 1992.

When a viewer wants to access a web page or other resource on the World Wide Web, s/he normally begins either by typing the URL of the page into his or her web browser, or by following a hypertext link to that page or resource. The first step, behind the scenes, is for the server-name part of the URL to be resolved into an IP address by the global, distributed Internet database known as the Domain name system or DNS.

The next step is for an HTTP request to be sent to the web server at that IP address, for the page required. In the case of a typical web page, the HTML text, graphics and any other files that form a part of the page will be requested and returned to the client (the web browser) in quick succession. The web browser's job is then to render the page as described by the HTML, CSS and other files received, incorporating the images, links and other resources as necessary. This produces the on-screen 'page' that the viewer sees.

Most web pages will themselves contain hyperlinks to other relevant and informative pages and perhaps to downloads, source documents, definitions and other web resources. Such a collection of useful, related resources, interconnected via hypertext links, is what has been dubbed a 'web' of information. Making it available on the Internet produced what Tim Berners-Lee first called the World Wide Web in the early 1990s.

If the user returns to a page fairly soon, it is likely that the data will not be retrieved from the source web server, as above, again. By default, browsers cache all web resources on the local hard drive. An HTTP request will be sent by the browser that asks for the data only if it has been updated since the last download. If it has not, the cached version will be reused in the rendering step. This is particularly valuable in reducing the amount of web traffic on the internet.

The decision about expiry is made independently for each resource (image, stylesheet, JavaScript file etc, as well as for the HTML itself). Thus even on sites with highly dynamic content, many of the basic resources are only supplied once per session or less. It is worth any web site designer collecting all the CSS and JavaScript into a few site-wide files so that they can be downloaded into users' caches and reduce page download times and demands on the server.

There are other components of the internet that can cache web content. The most common in practice are often built into corporate and academic firewalls where they cache web resources requested by one user for the benefit of all. Apart from the facilities built into web servers that can ascertain when physical files have been updated, it is possible for designers of dynamically generated web pages to control the HTTP headers sent back to requesting users, so that pages are not cached when they should not be – for example internet banking and news pages. This helps with understanding the difference between the HTTP 'GET' and 'POST' verbs – data requested with a GET may be cached, if other conditions are met, whereas data obtained after POSTing information to the server usually will not.

The Web can be traced back to a project at CERN in 1989 when Tim Berners-Lee and Robert Cailliau built ENQUIRE (short for *Enquire Within Upon Everything*, a book Berners-Lee recalled from his youth). While it was rather different from the Web we use today, it contained many of the same core ideas (and even some of the ideas of Berners-Lee's next project, the Semantic Web). Berners-Lee mentions that much of the motivation behind the project was so that he could access library information that was scattered on several different servers at CERN.

The primary underlying concept of hypertext came from earlier efforts, such as Ted Nelson's Project Xanadu and Douglas Engelbart's oN-Line System (NLS). The World Wide Web had a number of differences from other hypertext systems that were then in place.

– The WWW required only unidirectional links rather than bidirectional ones. This made it possible for someone to link to another resource without action by the owner of that resource. It also significantly reduced the difficulty of implementing Web servers and browsers (in comparison to earlier systems), but in turn presented the chronic problem of broken links.

- Unlike certain applications such as HyperCard or Gopher, the World Wide Web was non-proprietary, making it possible to develop servers and clients independently and to add extensions without licensing restrictions.

Screenshot of the very first WWW browser running on a NeXT system The initial "www" program at CERN displayed styled text and images, and it was a WYSIWYG HTML editor as well as the browser. As it ran only on NeXT machines, CERN released a simple, text-only version to the world. Some journalists first encountered the Web through the text browser written by Nicola Pellow and this engendered a myth that the Web was text-only until Mosaic came along. The Web had graphics from the start, at least for NeXT users. However, Mosaic did introduce the ability to combine text and images in a single page.

Java and JavaScript

Another significant advance in the technology was Sun Microsystems' Java programming language, which enabled web servers to embed small programs (called applets) directly into the information being served that would run on the user's computer, allowing faster and richer user interaction. JavaScript, however, is a scripting language that was developed for Web pages. While its name is similar to Java it was developed by Netscape and not Sun Microsystems. In conjunction with the Document Object Model, JavaScript has become a much more powerful language than its creators originally envisioned. Sometimes its usage is expressed under the term DHTML, or *Dynamic HTML,* to emphasise a shift away from *static* HTML pages.

The exponential growth of the Internet was primarily attributed to the emergence of the web browser Mosaic, followed by its commercial offspring Netscape Navigator, during the mid-1990s. It brought unprecedented attention to the Internet from media, industries, policy makers, and the general public. Eventually, it led to several visions of how our society might change, although some point out that those visions are not unique to the Internet, but repeated with many new technologies (especially information and communications technologies) of various era. Because the web is global in scale, some suggested that it will nurture mutual understanding on a global scale.

The web is available to individuals outside mass media. In order to "publish" a web page, one does not have to go through a publisher or other media institution, and potential readers could be found in all corners of the globe. Unlike books and documents, hypertext does not have a linear order from beginning to end. It is not broken down into the hierarchy of chapters, sections, subsections, etc. Many different kinds of information are now available on the web, and for those who wish to know other societies, their cultures and peoples, it has become easier.

Although some websites are available in multiple languages, many are in the local language only. Also, not all software supports all special characters, and RTL languages. These factors would challenge the notion that the World Wide Web will bring a unity to the world. The increased opportunity to publish materials is certainly observable in the countless personal pages, as well as pages by families, small shops, etc., facilitated by the emergence of free web hosting services.

Frustration over congestion issues in the Internet infrastructure and the high latency that results in slow browsing has lead to an alternative name for the Web: the *World Wide Wait*. Speeding up the Internet is an ongoing discussion over the use of peering and QoS technologies. Other solutions to reduce the World Wide Wait can be found on W3C

XHTML

Beginning XHTML covers media types, CSS2 and, of course, the relationship of both to XHTML. The World Wide Web is a wonderful thing: computers all over the world—connected together—sharing documents and multimedia. In recent years, the World Wide Web has begun to grow beyond this comfy computer-based family of devices. The Web is now accessible on mobile phones, handheld digital assistants, and televisions. This phenomenon has placed a considerable burden on content authors. No longer can they write their documents with expectations on how that content will be displayed.

Each of these new devices represents a quite different medium from the computer: the physical characteristics of the devices are different, the relationship between the device and the user is different, and the cost of using the device is different. Until recently, authors had little choice but to author or re-author their content with each device in mind. With the advent of Cascading Style Sheets (CSS) and something called 'media types,' this began to change.

One of the most exciting things about writing XHTML is that whatever you write can be viewed anywhere in the world, regardless of the type of computer being used to view the content. This means that whatever content you write, you had better be prepared for it to be viewed on any number of computers, television set-top boxes, game consoles, handheld digital assistants, and mobile phones. This would be quite a chore had HTML continued its evolutionary path of including presentational elements like <b> for bold and <center> for alignment.

The second mechanism for associating style sheets with media types is to use the <link> element's media attribute, which specifies the intended destination media for the external style information. This allows user agents to load and apply external style sheets based on the characteristics of the media where the document is being rendered.

The third mechanism for associating style sheets with media types is to use the @media rules. This specifies the target media types for a set of style sheet rules.

Properties of Style Sheet

Not every style sheet property is appropriate for every target device. The volume property, for example, refers to what's known as the median volume of a waveform. This property is clearly related to aural media types (i.e. sound) and not to visually oriented media types. In fact, it turns out that there are relationships between the different media types. These relationships are called media groups, and the World Wide Web Consortium identifies four of these media groups:

- Continuous or paginated media
- Visual, aural, or tactile media
- Grid or bitmap media
- Interactive or static media

Each media type is a member of one or more of these media groups. For example, the screen media type is a member of the continuous, visual, bitmap, interactive, and static media groups. Continuous or paginated media refers to the surface on which content is rendered. If the surface can always extend to hold all of the content, the media is considered continuous. If the surface has a limited size and additional surfaces must be created to hold all of the content, the media is said to be paginated. Computer screens are continuous and printed pages are paginated. Visual, aural, or tactile media refers to how the information is presented to the user:

- If the user must use their eyes to consume the content, then the media is said to be visual.
- If the user must use their ears to consume the content, then the media is said to be aural.
- If the user must use touch to consume the content, then the media is said to be tactile.

Computer screens are visual, aural browsers are aural, and Braille printers are tactile. Grid or bitmap media refers to how the visual or tactile information is rendered. If the information is rendered in a predefined grid layout (every 'character' has the same amount of space), then the media is said to be grid-based. If the information is rendered pixel by pixel (every 'character' uses whatever space it needs), then the media is said to be bitmap-based. Teletypes are grid-based and computer screens are bitmap-based.

Interactive or static media refers to whether the user can interact with the content. As would be expected, when the user can interact with the content, the media is said to be interactive. When the user cannot interact with the content, the media is said to be static. Computer screens are said to be interactive and printed pages are said to be static. Each Cascading Style Sheet property is only valid for one or more media groups. When you are tailoring a presentation to a particular media type, you need to identify the appropriate media group and determine whether you can control the desired property for that media group.

URI

URI is an agreement about how the Internet community

allocates names and associates them with the resources they identify. By design a URI identifies one resource. We do not limit the scope of what might be a *resource*. The term "resource" is used in a general sense for whatever might be identified by a URI. It is conventional on the hypertext Web to describe Web pages, images, product catalogues, etc. as "resources". The distinguishing characteristic of these resources is that all of their essential characteristics can be conveyed in a message. This set as *"information resources."*

However, the term resource is intentionally more broad. Other things, such as cars and dogs, are resources too. They are not information resources, however, because their essence is not information. Although it is possible to describe a great many things about a car or a dog in a sequence of bits, the sum of those things will invariably be an approximation of the essential character of the resource. We define the term "information resource" because we observe that it is useful in discussions of Web technology and may be useful in constructing specifications for facilities built for use on the Web.

Since the scope of a URI is global, the resource identified by a URI does not depend on the context in which the URI appears. URIs are divided into schemes that define, via their scheme specification, the mechanism by which scheme-specific identifiers are associated with resources. For example, the "http" URI scheme uses DNS and TCP-based HTTP servers for the purpose of identifier allocation and resolution. Just as one might wish to refer to a person by different names (by full name, first name only, sports nickname, romantic nickname, and so forth), Web architecture allows the association of more than one URI with a resource. URIs that identify the same resource are called *URI aliases*.

Collision

By design, a URI identifies one resource. Using the same URI to directly identify different resources produces a *URI collision*. Collision often imposes a cost in communication due to the effort required to resolve ambiguities. Suppose, for example, that one organisation makes use of a URI to refer to the movie *The Sting*, and another organisation uses the same URI to refer to a discussion forum about *The Sting*. To a third party, aware of both organisations, this collision creates confusion about what the URI identifies, undermining the value of the URI.

If one wanted to talk about the creation date of the resource identified by the URI, for instance, it would not be clear whether this meant "when the movie was created" or "when the discussion forum about the movie was created." Social and technical solutions have been devised to help avoid URI collision. However, the success or failure of these different approaches depends on the extent to which there is consensus in the Internet community on abiding by the defining specifications. URIs are sometimes used for indirect identification. This does not necessarily lead to collisions.

Allocation

URI allocation is the process of associating a URI with a resource. Allocation can be performed both by resource owners and by other parties. It is important to avoid URI collision.

Ownership

URI ownership is a relation between a URI and a social entity, such as a person, organisation, or specification. URI ownership gives the relevant social entity certain rights, including:

- to pass on ownership of some or all owned URIs to another owner—delegation; and
- to associate a resource with an owned URI—URI allocation.

By social convention, URI ownership is delegated from the IANA URI scheme registry [IANASchemes], itself a social entity, to IANA-registered URI scheme specifications. Some URI scheme specifications further delegate ownership to subordinate registries or to other nominated owners, who may further delegate ownership. In the case of a specification, ownership ultimately lies with the community that maintains the specification. The approach taken for the "http" URI scheme, for example, follows the pattern whereby the Internet community delegates authority, via the IANA URI scheme registry and the DNS, over a set of URIs with a common prefix to one particular owner. One consequence of this approach is the Web's heavy reliance on the central DNS registry.

A different approach is taken by the URN Syntax scheme which delegates ownership of portions of URN space to URN Namespace specifications which themselves are registered in an IANA-maintained registry of URN Namespace Identifiers. URI owners are responsible for avoiding the assignment of equivalent URIs to multiple resources. Thus, if a URI scheme specification does provide for the delegation of individual or organised sets of URIs, it should take pains to ensure that ownership ultimately resides in the hands of a single social entity.

Allowing multiple owners increases the likelihood of URI collisions. URI owners may organise or deploy infrastruture to ensure that representations of associated resources are available and, where appropriate, interaction with the resource is possible through the exchange of representations. There are social expectations for responsible representation management by URI owners.

Some schemes use techniques other than delegated ownership to avoid collision. For example, the specification for the data URL (sic) scheme specifies that the resource identified by a data scheme URI has only one possible representation. The representation data makes up the URI that identifies that resource. Thus, the specification itself determines how data URIs are allocated; no delegation is possible. Other schemes rely on a social process.

Comparisons

URIs that are identical, character-by-character, refer to the same resource. Since Web Architecture allows the association of multiple URIs with a given resource, two URIs that are not character-by-character identical may still refer to the same resource. Different URIs do not necessarily refer to different resources but there is generally a higher computational cost to determine that different URIs refer to the same resource. To reduce the risk of a false negative (i.e., an incorrect conclusion that two URIs do not refer to the same resource) or a false positive (i.e., an incorrect conclusion that two URIs do refer to the same resource), some specifications describe equivalence tests in addition to character-by-character comparison.

URI Aliases

Although there are benefits (such as naming flexibility) to URI aliases, there are also costs. URI aliases are harmful when they divide the Web of related resources. A corollary of Metcalfe's Principle (the "network effect") is that the value of a given resource can be measured by the number and value of other resources in its network neighbourhood, that is, the resources that link to it.

The problem with aliases is that if half of the neighbourhood points to one URI for a given resource, and the other half points to a second, different URI for that same resource, the neighbourhood is divided. Not only is the aliased resource undervalued because of this split, the entire neighbourhood of resources loses value because of the missing second-order relationships that should have existed among the referring resources by virtue of their references to the aliased resource. A URI owner should not associate arbitrarily different URIs with the same resource.

URI consumers also have a role in ensuring URI consistency. For instance, when transcribing a URI, agents should not gratuitously percent-encode characters. An agent that receives a URI SHOULD refer to the associated resource using the same URI, character-by-character. When a URI alias does become common currency, the URI owner should use protocol techniques such as server-side redirects to relate the two resources. The community benefits when the URI owner supports redirection of an aliased URI to the corresponding "official" URI.

URI aliasing only occurs when more than one URI is used to identify the same resource. The fact that different resources sometimes have the same representation does not make the URIs for those resources aliases.

Representation Type and Internet Media Type

A *representation* is data that encodes information about resource state. Representations do not necessarily describe the resource, or portray a likeness of the resource, or represent the resource in other senses of the word "represent". Representations of a resource may be sent or received using interaction protocols. These protocols in turn determine the form in which representations are conveyed on the Web. HTTP, for example, provides for transmission of representations as octet streams typed using Internet media types. Just as it is important to reuse existing URI schemes whenever possible, there are significant benefits to using media typed octet streams for representations even in the unusual case where a new URI scheme and associated protocol is to be defined.

New protocols created for the Web should transmit representations as octet streams typed by Internet media types. The Internet media type mechanism does have some limitations. For instance, media type strings do not support versioning or other parameters. The Internet Media Type defines the syntax and semantics of the fragment identifier (introduced in Fragment Identifiers, if any, that may be used in conjunction with a representation.

The semantics of a fragment identifier are defined by the set of representations that might result from a retrieval action on the primary resource. The fragment's format and resolution are therefore dependent on the type of a potentially retrieved representation, even though such a retrieval is only performed if the URI is dereferenced. If no such representation exists, then the semantics of the fragment are considered unknown and, effectively, unconstrained.

Fragment identifier semantics are orthogonal to URI schemes and thus cannot be redefined by URI scheme specifications. Interpretation of the fragment identifier is performed solely by the agent that dereferences a URI; the fragment identifier is not passed to other systems during the process of retrieval. This means that some intermediaries in Web architecture (such as proxies) have no interaction with fragment identifiers and that redirection does not account for fragments.

Content Negotiation

Content negotiation refers to the practice of making available multiple representations via the same URI. Negotiation between the requesting agent and the server determines which representation is served. HTTP is an example of a protocol that enables representation providers to use content negotiation. Individual data formats may define their own rules for use of the fragment identifier syntax for specifying different types of subsets, views, or external references that are identifiable as secondary resources by that media type. Therefore, representation providers must manage content negotiation carefully when used with a URI that contains a fragment identifier.

Successful communication between two parties depends on a reasonably shared understanding of the semantics of exchanged messages, both data and metadata. At times, there may be inconsistencies between a message sender's data and metadata.

Agents must not ignore message metadata without the consent of the user. Furthermore, representation providers can help reduce the risk of inconsistencies through careful assignment of representation metadata (especially that which applies across representations). The accuracy of metadata relies on the server administrators, the authors of representations, and the software that they use. Practically, the capabilities of the tools and the social relationships may be the limiting factors.

The accuracy of these and other metadata fields is just as important for dynamic Web resources, where a little bit of thought and programming can often ensure correct metadata for a huge number of resources. Often there is a separation of control between the users who create representations of resources and the server managers who maintain the Web site software. Given that it is generally the Web site software that provides the metadata associated with a resource, it follows that coordination between the server managers and content creators is required. A URI owner may supply zero or more authoritative representations of the resource identified by that URI.

There is a benefit to the community in providing representations. A URI owner should provide representations of the resource it identifies. For example, owners of XML namespace URIs should use them to identify a namespace document. Just because representations are available does not mean that it is always desirable to retrieve them. In fact, in some cases the opposite is true. Dereferencing a URI has a (potentially significant) cost in computing and bandwidth resources, may have security implications, and may impose significant latency on the dereferencing application. Dereferencing URIs should be avoided except when necessary.

As is the case with many human interactions, confidence in interactions via the Web depends on stability and predictability. For an information resource, persistence depends on the consistency of representations. The representation provider decides when representations are sufficiently consistent. Although persistence in this case is observable as a result of representation retrieval, the term *URI persistence* is used to describe the desirable property that, once associated with a resource, a URI should continue indefinitely to refer to that resource.

A URI owner should provide representations of the identified resource consistently and predictably. URI persistence is a matter of policy and commitment on the part of the URI owner. The choice of a particular URI scheme provides no guarantee that those URIs will be persistent or that they will not be persistent. HTTP has been designed to help manage URI persistence.

For example, HTTP redirection permits servers to tell an agent that further action needs to be taken by the agent in order to fulfil the request. In addition, content negotiation also promotes consistency, as a site manager is not required to define new URIs when adding support for a new format specification. Protocols that do not support content negotiation (such as FTP) require a new identifier when a new data format is introduced. Improper use of content negotiation can lead to inconsistent representations.

Data Formats Specification

A data format specification (for example, for XHTML, RDF/XML, SMIL, XLink, CSS, and PNG) embodies an agreement on the correct interpretation of representation data. The first data format used on the Web was HTML. Since then, data formats have grown in number. Web architecture does not constrain which data formats content providers can use. This flexibility is important because there is constant evolution in applications, resulting in new data formats and refinements of existing formats.

Although Web architecture allows for the deployment of new data formats, the creation and deployment of new formats (and agents able to handle them) is expensive. Thus, before inventing a new data format (or "meta" format such as XML), designers should carefully consider re-using one that is already available. For a data format to be usefully interoperable between two parties, the parties must agree (to a reasonable extent) about its syntax and semantics. Shared understanding of a data format promotes interoperability but does not imply constraints on usage; for instance, a sender of data cannot count on being able to constrain the behaviour of a data receiver. Some characteristics of a data format that facilitate integration into Web architecture.

Binary data formats are those in which portions of the data are encoded for direct use by computer processors, for example 32 bit little-endian two's-complement and 64 bit IEEE double-precision floating-point. The portions of data so represented include numeric values, pointers, and compressed data of all sorts. A textual data format is one in which the data is specified in a defined encoding as a sequence of characters. HTML, Internet e-mail, and all XML-based formats are textual.

Increasingly, internationalised textual data formats refer to the Unicode repertoire [UNICODE] for character definitions. If a data format is textual that does not imply that it should be served with a media type beginning with "text/". Although XML-based formats are textual, many XML-based formats do not consist primarily of phrases in natural language. In principle, all data can be represented using textual formats. In practice, some types of content (e.g., audio and video) are generally represented using binary formats.

The trade-offs between binary and textual data formats are complex and application-dependent. Binary formats can be substantially more compact, particularly for complex pointer-rich data structures. Also, they can be consumed more rapidly by agents in those cases where they can be loaded into memory and used with little or no conversion. Textual formats are usually more portable and interoperable. Textual formats also have the considerable advantage that they can be directly read by human beings (and understood, given sufficient documentation). This can simplify the tasks of creating and maintaining software, and allow the direct intervention of humans in the processing chain without recourse to tools more complex than the ubiquitous text editor.

Finally, it simplifies the necessary human task of learning about new data formats; this is called the "view source" effect. It is important to emphasise that intuition as to such matters as data size and processing speed is not a reliable guide in data format design; quantitative studies are essential to a correct understanding of the trade-offs. Therefore, designers of a data format specification should make a considered choice between binary and textual format design.

In a perfect world, language designers would invent languages that perfectly met the requirements presented to them, the requirements would be a perfect model of the world, they would never change over time, and all implementations would be perfectly interoperable because the specifications would have no variability. In the real world, language designers imperfectly address the requirements as they interpret them, the requirements inaccurately model the world, conflicting requirements are presented, and they change over time.

As a result, designers negotiate with users, make compromises, and often introduce extensibility mechanisms so that it is possible to work around problems in the short term. In the long term, they produce multiple versions of their languages, as the problem, and their understanding of it, evolve. The resulting variability in specifications, languages, and implementations introduces interoperability costs. Extensibility and versioning are strategies to help manage the natural evolution of information on the Web and technologies used to represent that information.

3

Media Convergence

Digital media of course plays a role in every communication function that analog media plays, ranging from surveillance to entertainment. A 24/7 media environment is quickly emerging, if not already here. Newspapers have had to create policies so their online versions do not scoop their printed morning edition the next day-as much so they do not tip off their competitors as for not wanting to hurt their own newspaper sales. With cable TV there is of course 24-hour entertainment and news, and the always-on nature of the Internet has taught the public that they can obtain specific media content on demand as long as they are connected to the Internet.

Even media that we are accustomed to thinking of as "set" once created, such as magazines or books, can easily be updated at any time if they are distributed in digital form. A nonstop media environment, although increasing the opportunities for news, information, and entertainment, also has its negative side. With new messages being delivered all the time and a huge choice of media to interact with, it can be very easy to become distracted with flashy entertainment or essentially "drown" in information.

Pervasiveness of the Media

The pervasiveness of the media system means that wherever one goes, there is likely to be unprecedented access to mass communication. A new media pioneer who works as a civilian researcher in a naval research lab once remarked that he was leaving for a week's vacation in the Caribbean on an island where there was no Internet, no phone service, and no communication services of any kind. He had to escape. Unfortunately, with today's global satellite communications, it's not possible to truly "escape" anywhere on the planet. Increasingly portable media devices and flat-panel screen technology improvements also mean that we have a growing ability to take our media with us and access it (or have it thrust upon us) in places where we previously did not encounter media.

Displays in elevators are one example of how advertisers are using technology to reach a captive audience. Pervasive mass communication means better access to entertainment, commercial information, and news. Such access means there is at least the potential for a better-functioning democracy, because more information is available. Of course, better access may not come evenly to all or allow everyone to benefit equally from that access. Simply providing more information into the media system may often result in a widening, rather than a narrowing, of the gap in knowledge between those in high and low socioeconomic groups.

The convergence of digital media is leading to the development of a personal information space. A personal information space is a virtual location assembled and accessed online where an individual keeps data, or information. It is more than just a digital personal library, however. In a personal information space, one can process private voice, fax, and e-mail communications, and create, access, and store Web-based media content, including multimedia, all from any location around the world. No longer is one's personal information space limited by geography, time, or culture.

One can access a personal information space when mobile computing and communications devices are connected to global, wired, and wireless telecommunications networks. Increasingly, the personal information space is being integrated with public information space (i.e., the content generated by media organisations and others). Unfortunately, the personal information space is also subject to various threats and dangers, such as erosion of privacy, computer hackers, or technical failures.

It is necessary to understand the basic workings of digital and online technology for the same reasons that they are changing mass communication-they create functionalities that no other media has previously been able to do. Hyperlinks are a fairly simple, yet illustrative, example. Until the creation of hypertext transfer protocol (HTTP) in 1991 by Tim Berners-Lee, there was no such thing as hyperlinks except in the imaginations of some researchers. But after it was created and started being used by large numbers of people, new issues began to arise. Although in theory hyperlinks can take the user anywhere else on the Web, in practice many organisations have protested the practice of deep linking, or linking to one of the Web site's inside pages, such as a particular story. This is because commercial media sites charge advertising rates based on how many visitors come to their home pages, and deep linking skirts this. On the other hand, it does little use to provide a link with a specific story in mind only to send users to another Web site's homepage and make them find it themselves.

But some Web sites compiled links of other Web sites and put them under their own Web address, making it look like the content was theirs. Another issue has arisen regarding whether a hyperlink is a form of free speech Another issue has arisen regarding whether a hyperlink is a form of free speech or simply a device that takes a user elsewhere. The object of contention in this case was a computer program known as DeCSS, which enabled users to effectively copy DVDs. The judge ruled that it was illegal to not only publish the programme on the Web but also, more extraordinarily, to link to any Web site containing the illegal computer code.

However, simply writing the Web site address without actually linking to it would be protected as free speech. In the case of hyperlinks, without an understanding of how they work and what characteristics make them different from traditional media, it is impossible to fully understand how online media are changing the overall media framework economically, legally, and in terms of media use. The same reasoning can be applied to many aspects of online and digital media.

Prior to the era of the Internet, institutions or organisations that had computers had no simple way for the computers to communicate with each other, even if they were connected by a wire, as computers ran machine-specific languages and programmes that could not be understood by other computers. In 1969, the foundations for the Internet were laid when the Defense Advanced Research Projects Agency (DARPA) launched the Advanced Research Projects Agency network, or ARPAnet. ARPAnet was the first national computer network, connecting many universities around the country for advanced, high-speed computing applications and research.

It was not yet the Internet, but it was the beginning of online communications. But there was still no "common language," or protocol, that computers could use to easily transmit information via the network. Although it is difficult to pin down an exact date when the Internet officially started, in 1982 the Defense Department adopted TCP/IP as the basis for the ARPAnet. Moreover, at this time researchers began defining an "internet" (lower case i) as a connected set of networks using TCP/IP, and the "Internet" as a set of connected TCP/IP internets. Creating the World Wide Web For the first decade of the Internet's existence, its usage was limited largely to researchers.

Use of the Internet required knowledge of a variety of arcane commands and terminology. The limited, specialised nature of the Internet underwent a fundamental change in 1991 when Tim Berners-Lee, an MIT researcher at a physics laboratory in Switzerland, invented the World Wide Web and began to open the use of the Internet to a much wider set of users. The advent of the Web as a global publishing medium made possible the most fundamental shift in human communication since the advent of the printing press five centuries earlier.

The Web enabled easy many-to-many communication over distance and time. In addition, in contrast to traditional media of mass communication, anyone can create and publish on the Web for very little cost or expertise. The World Wide Web (WWW) is a subset of the Internet and is perhaps best described as a global electronic publishing medium accessed through the Internet.

Technically speaking, the Web is made up of an interconnected set of computer servers on the Internet that subscribe to a set of TCP/IP network interface protocols. These technical protocols include assigning to a Web site a Uniform Resource Locator (URL) based on its TCP/IP Internet address, which is the Web site address that Web users are familiar with. URLs include the instructions that are read by a Web browser, a navigational tool to travel the Web. A Web page is any document, or collection of content, that resides on a Web site. The content can take any form, including text, graphics, photographs, audio, video, or interactive features, such as surveys or discussion forums.

A Web site can consist of one page of content or many such pages and can include hyperlinks to other Web sites. Content on a Web page is tagged, or marked up, using what is known as hypertext markup language, or HTML, to format the content so it displays correctly on a screen. In addition, each document uses hypertext transfer protocol (HTTP), which enables the standardised transfer of text, audio, and video files, as well as e-mail from one address to another.

Another huge gain in making the Internet accessible to even more people was the creation in 1993 of Mosaic by Marc Andreeson, then at the National Center for SuperComputing Applications (NCSA) at the University of Illinois at Champaign-Urbana. Mosaic, which eventually became Netscape, provided a graphical user interface with the Web that computer users who had Macs or Windows PCs could quickly understand and use. Although GUI browsers Viola and Erwise were also created in 1992, by the end of the year Mosaic was being written about in mainstream media and became the most well-known Web browser. Microsoft created their own graphical browser, Internet Explorer (IE), in 1996 to compete with Netscape's browser, then called Netscape Navigator.

By offering Internet Explorer free and eventually bundling it with the Windows operating system, IE was able to become the dominant Web browser in only four years, with 75 percent usage compared to Netscape's 25 percent. In 1999 Netscape was bought by AOL, a year before AOL acquired Time Warner. As any regular Web user can attest, Web sites and text size often look different not only on different browsers but on different versions of the same browser. More advanced functions or codes on Web sites may not show up on earlier browser versions, thus making it difficult for Web designers and content companies to create Web sites that are consistent across the online audience.

Reflecting the continued dramatic, almost exponential growth of the Web, by 2001 millions of individuals and organisations had published "home pages" on the Web. With the cost barriers to entry in the global publishing arena removed or dramatically lowered, the Web for the first time brought press freedom to virtually any citizen with access to a computer and a phone line. Of course, more than half the world lack either or both of these, so we're still a long way off from realising the dream of fully democratic communications. Still, by comparison, only some 45 percent of households in the United States subscribe to a daily newspaper, whereas almost 60 percent of U.S. adults had Internet (and thereby Web) access as of June 2002.

In its broadest sense, the Internet encompasses virtually all other media, as well as a broad cross-section of human culture, commerce, and creation. Virtually anything one can think of almost certainly exists in some form on the Internet, from information in the Library of Congress to deliberately misleading information created by hate groups or individuals. As distinguished communications scholar Fred Williams once observed, "Going on the Internet is like going through someone else's trash." The Internet as we know it now is not controlled by any one person or organisation. It is a medium of multimodal (i.e., it involves the various senses) content and interactive communications, in particular e-mail, where users (and organisations) send and receive text and increasingly audio, video, photos, graphics, and hyperlinks. Although much of the content on the Internet is available free to users, there is a growing trend among media and technology companies to start charging consumers, especially after advertising dropped off sharply after the dot-com meltdown in 2000.

Content or services that were previously free, such as a given amount of disk space or the ability to check remote e-mail accounts through Web e-mail accounts such as Hotmail, for example, were starting to be offered only to paying consumers. This trend of partially free services or content and payment for what is considered "premium" content can also be seen among media companies online, and it is still too early to tell whether these strategies will be successful in generating revenues. Online media companies are also experimenting with increasingly obtrusive online advertising, such as larger pop-up ad windows or automatic pop-under ads that are changing the look and experience of the Web for users. In the early 1990s there were many debates among users of online discussion groups about whether any advertising should even be allowed on the Internet, considering the fact that it was created by using taxpayers' money.

Computer Networks

Networks, or systems of interconnected communication vehicles, can take many forms. Networks have long been a fundamental part of mass communication, especially broadcasting. In broadcasting, networks of affiliated local stations provide a means of distributing shared programming to audiences across large geographic regions, most typically the entire country. Traditionally, these networks have been linked through analog technology. Today's networks are increasingly digital. This offers several advantages in mass communication, most importantly the ability to transmit multiple streams of information, including audio and video content, text, or other types of data. In addition, computer-based networks permit the distribution of content to be more flexible, so if one route of the network is unavailable, the network can automatically and efficiently reassemble through a different route.

Digital networks permit compression of data, which enables a mass communicator to send more information in the same amount of space on the network. Finally, a computer network easily permits downstream and upstream communications (from the source to the receiver, and vice versa), whereas traditional networks were largely one way and relatively expensive. A modem (a foreshortening of modulate-demodulate) is used to convert the digital information in a computer to analog signals for transmission over a phone or cable TV line and to convert analog signals to digital information for a computer.

Modems can also operate wirelessly by converting data into radio signals. Modems were invented in the 1960s, before the days of the personal computer, as a means of letting "dumb terminals" (i.e., electronic machines where users typed information on keyboards) dial into a remote computer. These early modems converted the typed characters into audio tones that were sent over the telephone line and then were converted back on the other end of the line where they were received by the computer, which processed the information received.

Today's modems operate in a much more efficient and faster fashion. Whereas early modems were hard-pressed to convert and transmit 300 bits per second, today's modems can convert and send millions of bits per second. This allows them to rapidly send or receive not just text but also audio and video.

Bandwidth Communication

Bandwidth is a crucial element for online communication to reach its full potential to be a mass medium. Without what is called high-speed, high-bandwidth, or broadband connections to the Internet, most people online are unable to receive audio or video in real time or at the same quality as they are used to from television or radio. Narrowband is the term used for low bandwidth communications, such as dial-up phone modems. Bandwidth available for Internet service has traditionally been narrowband via dial-up modems, typically delivering anywhere from 28 kilobits to 56 kilobits per second. Video at these narrowband rates is very limited, usually a small window of jerky motion, of low-resolution imagery and only marginally better sound.

In a technical sense, bandwidth refers to the electromagnetic frequency or spectrum available for delivering content. Bell Labs scientist Claude E. Shannon in 1948 provided a precise mathematical definition of bandwidth, defining the capacity of a communications channel in terms of bits per second. A voice phone call, for example, uses about 3000 hertz (Hz) bandwidth, whereas a telephone modem operating at about 33.6 kilobits per second requires a little more bandwidth, or about 3200 Hz. Think of bandwidth not so much as electromagnetic frequency, however, but more in terms of how large a pipe is that comes to your home delivering data rather than a physical thing like water.

Someone who is able to tap the large "data pipe" directly can access the flow of data at equally high speeds. Sometimes this is called a "fat pipe." However, if the pipe that accesses the main pipes is very thin, data will come at only a trickle, no matter how fast his or her personal computer is. As of 2002, the Internet was relatively limited in terms of available bandwidth. It varied depending on how a user connected to the Internet, such as a telephone modem or a cable modem, although a second generation of the Internet known as Internet 2 brought 45,000 times more bandwidth.

At that time the Internet 2 was already providing a very high-speed connection among 170 universities. It promises in the future to bring such high-speed connectivity to a broader portion of society. One of the great challenges that cable and telephone providers have begun to solve in the past decade is the so-called "last mile" obstacle. For more than a decade, many cable and telephone companies have had considerable bandwidth available in their backbone or trunk lines but have run into a problem connecting these broadband facilities over the "last mile" to the end consumer. The cost of making these final connections has been prohibitive. But as the cost of the technology has fallen and various technological innovations have occurred, it has become increasingly feasible to provide the last-mile connections. When this is completed, it means that consumers will have the same broadband access that currently only large organisations have.

In the world of telephony, development of the digital subscriber line (DSL) has made it possible to use standard telephone wire, the twisted-pair copper wire in most homes, to provide relatively low-cost broadband capabilities in the home. Other emerging network technologies, such as a DSL (asymmetric DSL, which means high-speed downstream, much slower upstream), are also being deployed by the phone companies. Telephone companies have lagged somewhat behind in their delivery of highspeed Internet and broadband digital video services to the home, with DSL available in only a handful of markets.

Many customers have complained bitterly about late or no installation, technical troubles with little customer support, and lack of communication between the telephone companies and the Internet Service Providers (ISPs) that have hampered easy installation of DSL services. In the cable TV world, the cable modem and the set-top box have made it practical for many cable systems to begin rolling out digital cable services that not only provide digital TV programme services to the home but also permit highspeed Internet access and telephone service.

Broadband content delivery via already existing coaxial cable systems mean that cable modems are roughly 174 times faster than 56k modems. One problem of the cable modem is that the network is not switched; the network bandwidth is shared by the users within each local geographic area, or node. In other words, the more users on a given cable modem node, the slower the network becomes. Cable companies can put fewer users on nodes by increasing the number of nodes, but this of course increases their costs. TCI has already indicated that movies on demand or video on demand will be limited in its cable modem service to about 15 minutes in duration.

Bandwidth availability is gradually increasing as low-cost bandwidth rolls out nationwide in the first years of the twenty-first century and low-cost digital consumer access devices enter the marketplace. The importance of broadband capability to usage patterns on the Internet may be profound. Research shows that Internet users with broadband access already have substantially different behaviours than when they used dial-up connections. One trend that has been noted is that they are more likely to create and distribute media content than dial-up users. Online expenditures more than double for users of broadband services.

David Clark says that broadband Internet could bring "Real-time high-fidelity music, telephone, videoconferencing, television and radio programmes.... There will be new entertainment options, such as movies-on-demand, and new features, such as the ability to call up information about a movie's director or its actors as they appear on screen. Users will be able to play online games-live-against many contestants scattered around the globe." Of course, the data on high-bandwidth users are hard to interpret, because those who have access to broadband capabilities in 2002 are, in general, what are called "early adopters." They tend to have more income, are more educated, and are likely to be two-parent households. They are different by nature than the late adopters, and it may be in part these differences that account for the differences in how they connect to the Internet.

Many mass communication sites originally created solely online are also available, from one-person operations to major endeavors by large companies such as Microsoft in their creation of the online magazine Slate. Even companies not traditionally involved with mass communication have found that maintaining their own Web sites is an excellent way to communicate directly to a large audience.

Advantages of Digital Books

Digital books offer a variety of advantages over printed books, including permitting the reader not only to read the text but to make electronic annotations and bookmarks, access the content of the book via an interactive table of contents, and keyword search the entire text. Digital books and their sale online also point to a fundamental issue in the future of how mass communication industries will derive much if not most of their revenue: from online transactions, or what is called e-commerce. Although few people still may want to read a book on a standard computer screen, the Internet has brought a growing number of books online and made them available universally.

Much of the content of these online books may be most valuable as a research tool, but many may also find them a potentially viable way to read for pleasure. Segments of a book can be printed out, for example, saving weight and space when travelling, and as computer screen technology gets better and creates sharper images, reading on-screen will not be as tiring as it can be today. In the late 1990s, major publishers prepared for a growing surge in consumer demand for electronic books, and many experimented with the online sale and distribution of digital books.

However, after the economic slowdown in 2000, which hit technology and Internet companies particularly hard, and a subsequent slowdown in sales of digital books, publishers started to adopt a slower, more cautious approach. However, many believe that just as young people powered the paperback revolution, the young are showing a voracious appetite for digital books.

Online Newspaper

Newspapers are among the leading providers of online news. Online newspaper sites also face direct competition on a number of other fronts in the online arena, including to some degree the general public, who can put online eyewitness accounts of events. Matt Drudge's site was ranked twentieth in August 2002 of top news sites. News services such as AP or Reuters offer their breaking news content online on news aggregator/portal sites such as Yahoo! News, which was in third place.

Newspaper Web sites have the potential to take back some of the ground in breaking news coverage that they lost to television, but this can create an odd situation of a newspaper Web site "scooping" its more established print version, which comes out on a set schedule. The competition online newspapers face with cable and broadcast television news channels shows in part the complexity of the online mass communication world.

Advertising is another big area in which newspaper companies are threatened by the Internet, especially classified ads. Classified ads make up a large portion of advertising revenues for most newspapers, but online classified ads aggregators can allow people to search far more ads than are usually covered in a newspaper's circulation area. If a consumer wants to look for an item in a region that is covered by four or five different newspapers, there is no reason for that person to go to each newspaper's Web site to look at classifieds when he or she can see them all on one Web site. Likewise, a consumer can visit an online auction site like eBay and reach a nationwide group of potential sellers or buyers.

Digital Magazines

Despite the low bandwidth requirements for online text, online magazines have not been very successful to date. There are very few purely online magazines, Slate.com and Salon.com being two of the most prominent ones, but even these two online magazines have not been profitable despite publishing articles from world-class writers. Print-based magazines have done little original online content, preferring to use online versions of their magazines mainly for promoting print stories or archiving past issues.

There are several likely reasons that online magazines have fared poorly, despite the apparent benefits the online world would seem to bring to magazines and long-form nonfiction writing in particular because of the lack of space limitations. One of the main reasons is technological; reading long blocks of text on computer monitors becomes tiresome because the resolution of computer monitors has not reached the same quality as text on a printed page. Even once computer monitors do achieve higher resolutions, there is still the issue of portability. In other words, unless monitors can compete with a printed magazine in terms of clarity and portability (and to some extent disposability), there is likely to be a barrier among people in reading anything of any length in a digital format. This of course is not unique to magazines, as digital books and newspapers face the same issues.

E-ink or some other digital form of paper may solve this problem, but this will not reach consumers for a few years yet. With greater competition for their attention during the day, the public seems less willing to spend the time necessary to read long articles. In an online environment, readers are also more likely to click on hyperlinks to get more information rather than wait for the author to fully explain a point. Likewise, an article may be a starting point for a much more robust discussion among Web users in the form of online discussion groups.

However, there could be an important niche for magazines to provide a measure of distance and perspective on issues and to thereby be a voice of authority in their specialised area. If a magazine is perceived as having suitable authority and is respected highly enough by its readers, it seems that the public is willing to pay for online subscriptions. Consumer Reports Online is one of the few success stories in the online magazine world, with over 580,000 subscribers who can access archived articles and reviews on various products.

Digital Music

The MP3 file format represents an interesting example to illustrate how the new networked digital marketplace works. It's indicative how the recording industry is likely to sell much of its music in the future. The $5 billion recording industry is faced with a dramatic shift as users embrace digital audio and all the flexibility and power it affords them. The MP3 file format is used to compress near-CD-quality audio of music, which then lets the files, which generally range between 2 and 4 MB in size, be distributed easily over the Internet. There is nothing inherently illegal in the MP3 file format itself; it is simply the technology used to compress audio files.

The problems with the recording industry arise because consumers can copy, download, and distribute music largely for free through file-swapping services such as KaZaA. The recording industry has long held that it is acceptable for an individual who purchases an album, cassette, or CD to make a copy for personal use, and it is of course not uncommon for friends to exchange copies of music among themselves. File-sharing of online music takes these exchanges to completely new levels, however.

At any given time during the day, it is not unusual for 1.8 million users to be on a service such as KaZaA, exchanging close to 300 million files. These are not simply audio, of course, and can include video, text, and images as well, but it would be safe to say most of the files being shared are music files. KaZaA, Morpheus, Grokster, the now-defunct Napster, and many other online peer-to-peer file sharing systems have been at the core of this phenomenon. For now, suffice it to say that the major labels and everyone else in the recording industry value chain are enormously threatened by this development. They lose significant control and, they say, their profits and investments are being reduced along with the piracy of their intellectual property. As production and distribution costs decrease, more people can create their own professional-sounding (although not necessarily good) recordings and distribute them digitally. One solution that is emerging is the use of intelligent agent-based collaborative filtering, a sort of music club for the digital age.

Online Radio

Music is one of the most popular forms of online entertainment. Thousands of radio stations offer live webcasts of their regular over-the-air transmissions, although there are unsettled issues regarding royalty payments for webcasts of recorded music. In 2002, the U.S. Copyright Office decided that webcasters must pay 70 cents per song heard by 1000 listeners, half of what a government panel recommended they pay in a decision in February 2000 but still less than what the recording industry was asking.

Webcasters also have to pay royalties retroactively from 1998, and many of them said the rates and retroactive payments would cost them hundreds of thousands of dollars and force them to shut down. Traditional radio stations are exempt from this new royalty payment method, successfully arguing in 1998 that they are helping promote the music. The term radio is itself somewhat meaningless in an online digital world in which music is not broadcast over the air but retrieved by users on demand over the Internet.

In that way, online "radio" is technically audio programming, and in some ways will seem much closer to the current state of on-demand online music downloads, even though the term radio may stay with us or change its meaning. Regardless of the technical approach, online-only radio stations such as spinner. com are free of many FCC regulations and don't require a license to operate. Moreover, they reach a global audience, and there's no potential for signal interference. As a result, there are hundreds, possibly thousands of online radio stations.

Many of these stations operate independently of any broadcast parent, although legislation is being drafted that will bring them under some of the same rules broadcasters face. Online radio stations must abide by the Digital Millennium Copyright Act, however, which prohibits the advance posting of playlists, which would permit users to plan in advance when to copy songs. Even before the 2002 rulings on royalty payments for webcasts, some online radio stations paid royalties to one of the two music licensers in the United States, the American Society of Composers, Authors and Publishers (ASCAP), or Broadcast Music Inc. (BMI).

Live transmissions of sports events have emerged as an important part of online radio. In the case of major league baseball, Internet users must pay a fee ($14.95 in 2002) to listen to live audio webcasts of professional baseball games. Some other professional sports, such as the National Football League (NFL), make the audiocasts of their games available for free online. One of the challenges of listening to online radio is finding stations that are available. One list with more than 10,000 Internet radio stations from all around the world was created by WMBR-FM at the Massachusetts Institute of Technology. It allows for searches by country or region, call letters, format, or frequency.

Digital Film

The Internet has proven a valuable means of distribution for film, especially independent and short films, which have traditionally found distribution to be the most vexing bottleneck in becoming successful. Because independent and short films vary widely in quality and style and are produced outside the mainstream of Hollywood, few theaters, or theater chains, have been interested in showing them. Because of the low cost of online distribution and the potential to build audiences over time and space, a growing number of Web sites provide extensive independent and short films online, typically for free viewing. Two of the leading independent film sites are Indie Films and ifilm. These advertising and e-commerce-supported sites feature hundreds of independent films and film trailers for free viewing.

BMW Films is another interesting example of an online film site, in this case funding the production of independent short films-as long as all funded and shown films feature BMW cars. As commercially oriented as this may sound, the films produced have been of very high quality and not too crass in their commercialism. The quality of the online films available on the site, some done by famous directors, have been praised widely by leading independent critics.

Online Television

There is a wide variety of sources of video content online. Most television stations and all major networks maintain Web sites. A small but growing number of them provide at least some of their programming via the Web. An even smaller but growing number of these and other programmers provide near-broadcast quality video programming via the Web, some of it on demand. Viewers can go to the station's Web site and select from a variety of news and information options, including stories reported in text, audio, or video format. These various formats help add depth to the stories that video-only formats simply are not able to do because of the need for interesting visuals, sometimes at the expense of exploring related issues to a story. For established broadcast or cable stations, changing to a digital format that allows them to take full advantage of the capabilities of online video can be expensive.

Television programming typically has been provided to the public by a limited set of programme providers. They have made their programming available on a scheduled basis, packaged for mass audiences and broadcast according to a controlled schedule. Just as online music distribution opens the music recording industry to potentially thousands of new artists (i.e., programme providers), the Internet opens the TV business to thousands, perhaps millions, of new TV programme providers.

Internet-original programming began with web cams, tiny cameras that attach to a computer that have enjoyed enormous popularity around the world. Web cams have provided typically live feeds of everything from a coffee pot at Oxford University to a seemingly endless series of individuals inviting the public to pay to watch their uncensored private lives. This early experimentation among amateurs has given rise to much more serious original online video programming, however. Some of the most interesting are web cams set up by researchers to allow viewers from around the world to observe important, unusual, or simply interesting experiments or other research in action.

Universities and not-for-profit organisations have also used online video to show lectures from famous guest speakers, panel discussions, or to highlight on-the-scene video footage shot elsewhere in the world that does not make it to mainstream media. The same developments that have challenged the recording industry will start to emerge in the television industry as digital television enters the marketplace and broadband use increases, allowing for fast downloads of large files.

Digital video files are much larger than what most people can accommodate in downloads, which has hampered the popularity of video file-swapping online. Fixed media, such as videotapes or DVDs, are still primarily used for on-demand, repeated viewing, although new technologies could easily change this as well and make fixed media obsolete. The television industry has been closely watching what the recording industry is doing with the hope that they will not repeat the same mistakes. However, concerns about intellectual property theft and unwanted competition have limited some programmers' forays online.

Large television companies, broadcasters, and cable companies generally see the Internet and digital video as threatening their loss of control and their existing franchises, and whether they learn from the experiences of the recording industry or follow them in litigation and political lobbying to stop potential threats to their control remains to be seen. So far, attempts at creating secure digital media have not been successful. They have either been extremely clumsy and overly restricted consumers' ability to play media such as a CD on a variety of devices, have been foiled by low-tech mechanisms such as using a black marker pen to mask digital encoding, or have been extremely unpopular with consumers and thus failed, such as what happened with the DIVX format that forced consumers to pay per use of a digital video they "bought."

Traditionally, media enterprises, like other industrial-age businesses, required heavy capital investment. Capital was required to build the transmission towers for television and radio stations. It was required to buy printing presses and to build cable systems. Not only was the infrastructure expensive, but it created enormous barriers to entry for prospective competition. In the digital age, these rules are changing. Some of the most significant barriers to entry are shrinking. Capital costs are reduced, as anyone can go online and create a Web site and potentially compete with established media companies.

Of course, the cost of producing quality original content is still relatively high, especially for video but less so for text or audio. Moreover, few media enterprises have found a formula for making profits in the online world, as most people seem unwilling to pay for content and advertising does not seem to be very effective.

Most large online media outlets have the backing of traditional media companies behind them, such as MSNBC.com, a joint venture between NBC and Microsoft, or CNBC.com. With advertising and other revenues being generated from the parent companies, these online endeavors can afford to take losses for a while as online revenue models can be tried and tested. Many smaller, independent media dot-com companies were not so fortunate, especially after the economy and stock market spiralled downward from spring 2000.

Convergence of Telecommunications

There is perhaps no better example of how convergence of telecommunications companies and media companies is affecting mass communication than AOL Time Warner. America Online is the world's largest online communications service provider, with 34 million subscribers as of July 2002 and localised versions of AOL in eight languages in 17 countries. There are 120 million registered users of its popular instant messaging service, ICQ, which is available to non-AOL Internet users as well. AOL operates a unique, proprietary online communications service based on its own computer software authoring environment, as well as providing access to the Internet. This makes it the world's largest ISP as well.

Founded in 1985, the Dulles, Virginia-based firm in 1998 acquired the number-two ISP, Compuserve, which was among the earliest online services along with its then 2 million customers (now 3 million). In 1999, AOL acquired Netscape, a popular Web browser with 48 million users, positioning AOL for global leadership in the Internet and online communications markets. It also put the company in direct competition with Microsoft, which has the leading Web browser, Internet Explorer, and operates its own ISP, Microsoft Network (MSN).

AOL provides its members (what AOL calls its subscribers) with a wide variety of online services, including e-mail, Web browsing, online shopping, and instant messaging. In addition, AOL provides extensive content channels, including news, sports, and entertainment. Most content is provided to AOL by a variety of media content producers, including CNN, CBS News, and the Associated Press (AP). Entertainment content providers include TV Guide, EW.com (Entertainment Weekly), E Online, and People, while music and music-related news and entertainment is provided by sources such as Rolling Stone and Sonicnet.

AOL does produce some original content, mostly through its AOL TV, which is distributed both online and via DBS provider DirecTV. Mostly, though, AOL offers its users a convenient, user-friendly bundle of content and services packaged uniquely for AOL's members. An example would be AOL's nicely produced special interactive section on the 2001 Emmy Awards. It featured extensive coverage on the nominees, including text, audio, and video. All this comes at a price, with subscribers paying an annual fee of about $270, or a monthly rate of about $25.

Importantly, AOL is easy to install and use, making it a popular service among less technologically sophisticated users and leading to the charge by critics of AOL that it is "the Internet on training wheels." However, predictions by Internet pundits that once users became accustomed to being online they would then leave AOL and its pop-up ads in droves have not come true, although AOL's rate of growth in getting new subscribers has fallen off markedly in the past couple of years.

Microsoft

Most computer users look at and use Microsoft products. Although Microsoft is still primarily a technology or Internet company, its forays into content creation and development make it a potentially powerful force in the world of digital media. A merger with a media giant that has lots of content, such as Sony or Viacom, would create a media monolith along the lines of AOL Time Warner. Microsoft is involved in every aspect of the technology behind content creation and distribution on the Internet. Its Windows Media Player to watch or listen to streaming media was created to compete with RealNetworks RealPlayer and Apple's QuickTime.

Microsoft started integrating its Windows Media Player into its Windows operating system, making it easy for consumers to use. Because Windows Media Player is incompatible with either of the other two proprietary streaming media formats, however, streaming content creators have to duplicate their streaming content for all formats if they want to reach the largest possible audience, which increases production costs. Hardware makers and media content companies in television and Hollywood are wary of relying on a single proprietary standard, however, and are likely to put pressure on streaming media makers to use an open, common standard such as MPEG-4, although these issues are still unresolved.

Microsoft is also an ISP, with its MSN network, and is increasing its broadband capabilities. Its Net Passport services attempt to give Internet users an easy way to access various types of content and to conduct e-commerce in a secure environment. In a partnership with NBC, Microsoft is part of cable channel and popular news Web site MSNBC. They have started competing with video game makers with their Xbox video game console and have been involved in development of interactive television, first with WebTV and then with UltimateTV, but cut back on research in the area as of early 2002 as their interactive television ventures had not met with great success.

RealNetworks makes the popular RealPlayer software that lets consumers locate and listen to streaming audio and video over the Internet. More than 250 million people have downloaded RealPlayer to stream audio, video, and other multimedia content. It used to be the dominant streaming media software, but Microsoft has made great inroads into its area by bundling its proprietary Windows Media Player for free into its operating system, much as they did with Internet Explorer when they started competing with Netscape's Web browser.

RealNetworks, although it still gets almost 60 percent of its sales from licensing its software to consumers and content providers, has also been striking deals with content providers such as MLB.com for the rights to stream games over the Internet. It is also embracing the open MPEG-4 video compression standard rather than its proprietary RealPlayer standard in order to better partner with mobile hardware production companies. Digitisation of media has lowered production costs and lessened training needed to create professional-quality media content (at least in terms of technical proficiency, if not always in terms of content quality).

The Internet has created a networked environment that lets anyone reach a potential audience of millions of people for very little cost. The changes have threatened and will continue to threaten the interests of many established media companies unless they learn to adapt to the changing media environment. Although rapid improvements in technology make it impossible to accurately predict what specific changes will affect media in the future, there are several basic trends that will influence online and digital media in the coming years. Some of these trends simply accelerate changes that have already been taking place with analog media, while others are unique to the digital, Internet-connected media world.

It is already very easy to become overwhelmed by the amount of media available, and this trend is only likely to increase. The media world has gone from one of scarcity, where it was difficult to find certain items like rare editions of books, film, or music, to a world in which more than you could ever want can be found largely online or, if not there, then the Internet can show you where to find it. Issues of space or time that publishers or broadcasters dealt with are no longer a factor online. There is no physical reason to cut a story to 300 words so it fits on a page, although there very well may be reasons of clarity or design to cut a story online.

Likewise, it does not matter if an online video segment is longer than three minutes, as there are no advertisers who will get angry that their ad was not broadcast at a certain commercial break. Of course, these analog media limitations can be, and in some cases have been, placed on digital media, but there is no inevitable law that says it must be so. What this means for media professionals is that they are no longer the gatekeepers of information, deciding what is deemed important enough, given limited resources, to be sent through the media system to be distributed to the public. Rather, they will be filters or matchmakers of information, processing the raw material that almost anyone can access, and shortening, clarifying, and putting it in a larger context for the audience. This means media consumers will need to become more discriminating about what media they consume so they do not waste time or drown in information overload. Technologies such as collaborative filtering are likely to play a role in helping bring only the type of media content that a person wants.

Audience Fragmentation

Just as magazine audiences fragmented with the advent of television, and broadcast television audiences fragmented with the advent of cable, audiences are fragmenting even further in an online environment. This audience fragmentation will have profound effects on advertising revenues, because under the current advertising-supported models media companies get more revenue when they can attract a larger audience. Greater fragmentation also means that it is less likely that large groups of people will share media experiences and will therefore have less in common than they otherwise would have. The flip side of that argument is that those who do interact with a group that shares their interest can perhaps feel closer to others than if they were in a more homogenised, less fragmented media world.

Costs have always been relatively low for writers-a typewriter, paper, and some perseverance, and a person could see his or her name in print fairly easily, even if the published work did not receive a wide distribution. Computers and word processing software of course helped this process. Video and television production, however, have been a different story until recently. At present, for less than $10,000 someone can buy all the necessary equipment (computer, camera, and software) to digitally edit video at professional levels of quality, suitable for broadcast by mainstream media. It may still seem like a lot of money, but considering that even 15 years ago the costs for a similar set-up were more along the lines of $100,000, costs have dropped considerably. This is not to say that anyone can-or should-plan to be a television producer simply because it's possible.

It takes practice and skill to learn to use technologically sophisticated equipment such as digital video cameras and computers proficiently, as well as learning the media grammar of video in terms of cuts, staging shots, and lighting. However, the fact that someone with the necessary training, practice, and skills can create something without years of apprenticeship in a traditional media company is a dramatic shift and will lead to more participation among the general public in creating and interacting with mass media. The relatively low costs to create and produce media such as music or video will open the field to many more people creating media content.

As with the textheavy Internet now, much of that content will not be very good, causing some to long for the days of gatekeepers such as strict editors and record label executives who screened the abysmal from the mediocre, but there will be many more voices available to be heard and seen that would have otherwise been silenced in the traditional media world, and some of these will be worth listening to or watching, even if they do not have mass-market appeal.

Broadband Connections

As broadband connections reach more and more households, the way the public uses the Internet will change. Online video and graphics will become a viable choice for receiving content, thereby changing the Web from its current text emphasis to a more visual, video-oriented medium. Text will still play a role, however, but could well be pushed to a largely secondary or supporting role when someone wants more in-depth content on a topic. Text will also continue on the Web simply because it is likely to be some time before broadband penetrates enough homes for content producers to ignore those with dial-up modems.

TV or PC Convergence

It is still unclear at this stage whether the television will absorb the PC or the PC will absorb the television; but there will increasingly be little difference between the two. When one can watch a rerun of Seinfeld on demand and can do instant messaging with friends or check e-mail on the same screen while watching it, it will matter little to consumers whether that device is defined as a PC or a TV, because it will function as both. Interactivity at some level will be an expected part of the "television" viewing experience, although there will also be times when the public are more than willing to be passive media consumers again and simply sit back and watch what they want.

But for media and technology companies, the direction in which the PC/TV goes can be a matter of success or failure. Where will computer maker Dell be, for example, if the public starts buying Sony equipment that meets their computing and entertainment-viewing needs? Video-on-demand will largely make the concept of programming at specific times obsolete, except for live shows, special events or breaking news. Audiences will not need to tune into a specific channel at a certain time to see a rerun of The Simpsons. It will, in a sense, always be "on"-just as all other episodes will be-all available from an on-screen menu that's keyword searchable and that lets you choose what show or shows you wish to see.

Challenges in Online Media

One of the most significant challenges all online media properties face is building a revenue stream not only to cover costs but to return a profit. There are several ways online media companies can generate revenues-at least in theory. These include traditional methods such as advertising, subscriptions, and syndication, as well as methods that are either unique or feasible in an online environment, such as e-commerce and micropayments. However, none so far have proven to be inherently better than other method, and dot-com companies as well as online media companies are still experimenting with methods to earn profits.

It is likely that more advanced technology will open the door to creative revenue generating models that are unavailable today. For the time being, the revenue streams that appear most viable for content sites involve a combination of advertising, subscription, and micropayments. AOL produces substantial revenues, but mostly from its monthly subscription fees, which are actually charges for online service rather than content per se. AOL does produce some revenue from online transactions in the form of online shopping. This may grow significantly in the future as more consumers become used to buying online. Advertising has proved disappointing in generating revenues for all but the largest portal or content sites, such as Yahoo! or MSNBC.com, which attract millions of visitors.

Media companies both offline and online charge advertisers for the cost per thousand (CPM) of audience members. This means a magazine with a circulation of 100,000 can receive more for carrying ads than a magazine with a circulation of 10,000. In the online media environment, technology allows Web site owners not only to see exactly how many people have visited a given page on the site but to track whether people clicked on the advertisement on that page or not. Because the average numbers of click throughs on ads are generally extremely low (ranging between 0.75 percent for standard banner ads to 1.5 percent for large oversize ads in the center of the screen), advertisers have become more cautious about placing their ads online based simply on the numbers of visitors to a site.

It may well be that ads are similarly ineffective in the analog world, but there is of course no way to measure that in the concrete terms that the online world can provide. Online companies have tried a number of things to improve click-through rates on ads and thereby increase revenues. Larger ads, animated ads, pop-up and pop-under ads have all been tried, but with minimal success. In fact, most computer users seem much less patient with advertising than they are on television probably overhyped in the late 1990s, it could be argued that it has likewise been looked at overly skeptically in the post-dot-com boom era.

Yet, e-commerce presents an interesting opportunity in the long run for media businesses operating in the digital age. The online arena is an environment in which consumers can not only get information about products on demand, but, conversely, media and other organisations can deliver promotional messages specifically targeted to individuals based on their online profiles. In many cases consumers can also purchase those products or services and even have them delivered digitally via the Internet, as is the case for music, computer software, digital books, videogames, and some other products. For those that can't be delivered electronically, most are shipped via commercial delivery services anywhere in the world.

A major issue for online media organisations is how to provide a secure environment for payments for online transactions. Many consumers are concerned about the safety of providing a credit card number via the Internet and thus are afraid of venturing online to make a purchase of any type. Another issue that online media organisations must consider when venturing into e-commerce is maintaining viewer trust in their content and disclosing potential conflicts of interest or even the appearance of conflicts of interest.

Industrial Challenge

Broadband digital media present both an opportunity and a threat for those in the media and communication industries. On the one hand, long-standing corporations, institutions, and entire industries are being turned upside down by the digital revolution. Businesses built on analog technologies of production and distribution are trying to figure out how to adapt in the digital age. New efficiencies of creating and delivering content in a digital, networked environment are emerging throughout the world.

Long-held, highly profitable business models based on the analog world are less viable in a digital marketplace. Yet, uncertainty prevails in the largely digital world. Dot-com stocks have plummeted. Converting to digital production and distribution costs a lot of money, and the returns are not guaranteed. No wonder so many executives in the media business are nervous about digitisation choice and change. Nevertheless, the new digital world means new business opportunities. It means opening new markets that formerly were restricted by political, economic, and geographic boundaries. It means new storytelling formats that bring true interactivity to television and radio.

It means creating immersive audio and video on demand for consumers who want their media, in all its forms, customised according not only to their preferences but also to their current geographic location and many other factors. Overall, the digitisation of television and radio means an expansion of the business pie. In other words, the size of the marketplace is growing, which means extraordinary business opportunities for those brave enough, talented enough, and persistent enough to enter the fray in a creative manner. Established businesses face the additional hurdle of having to deal with their own corporate culture that insists on placing a priority on protecting their existing business interests. This shortsighted thinking opens new opportunities for entrepreneurial startups nimble enough to adapt to an uncertain and rapidly changing marketplace.

4

Digital Communication

In order to understand the changes taking place in our information activities, it is vital to understand some of the underlying structures and principles of the digital world. All digital data, from whatever original it derives, has the same underlying structure, that of the 'bit' or the Binary digit. A bit is an electronic impulse that can be represented by two states, 'on' or 'off', also written as '1' or '0'.

A 'byte' consists of eight bits, and one byte represents one alphanumeric character. A ten-letter word, for example, would be ten bytes. Bits and bytes are linked together in chains of millions of electronic impulses; this is known as the 'bit stream'. A 'kilobyte' is 1024 bytes, and a 'megabyte' 1024 kilobytes.

Digital images are represented by 'pixels' or picture elements—dots on the computer screen or printed on paper. Pixels can carry a range of values, but at the simplest level, one pixel equals one bit, and is represented in binary form as 'black' (off) or 'white' (on). Images captured at this level are 'bi-tonal'—pure black and white. Images can also be represented as eight-bit images, which have 256 shades of either grey or colour, and 24-bit images, which have millions of colours—more than the eye can distinguish.

The number of bits chosen to represent each pixel is known as the 'bit depth', and devices capable of displaying and printing images at high bit depths (36 or 48 bits) are now emerging. Bit depth is the number of bits per pixel, 'resolution' is the number of pixels (or printed dots) per inch, known as ppi or dpi. The higher the resolution, the finer the texture of a digital image. The resolution of most computer screens is generally in the range of 75 to 150 pixels per inch. This is adequate for display purposes, but visual content at this resolution is inadequate for printing (especially in colour), though images of black and white printed text or line art are often acceptable.

Highdensity images of library originals (manuscripts, photographs, etc.) need to be captured in the range 300-600 ppi for print-quality output. Almost any kind of information can be represented in these seemingly simple structures, as patterns of the most intricate complexity can be built up. Most primary sources held in libraries and other cultural institutions are capable of digital representation (anything that can be photographed can be digitised, though there are issues with the faithful representation of 3-D objects).

When digital they are susceptible to manipulation, interrogation, transmission and cross-linking in ways that are beyond the capacity of analogue media. Creating an electronic photocopy of a plain page of text is not a sophisticated process compared with analogue technologies, but being able to then automatically recognise all the alphanumeric characters it contains, plus the structural layout and metadata elements, is sophisticated, and is only achievable in a digital environment. Alphanumeric symbols are the easiest objects to represent in digital form, and digital text has been around for as long as there have been stored-program computers. These symbols are also the most compact to store, an important factor at a time when capacity was limited and expensive.

Early computers were good at processing symbols rapidly, but input, output and display of data were difficult. Input was via punched cards or tapes, output through printers or plotters with limited capabilities, and display was limited to ASCII symbols, displayed line by line, often with only upper case available. Special fonts and characters were fearsomely difficult to represent, though some early pioneers made creative use of graph plotters for non-Roman character sets. Early digital character representations were sparse in their storage needs, and early computer programs economical in their need for processing power.

Storage and power have been increasing steadily over the past three decades, with the capacity of the processor chip doubling approximately every 24 months, much to the surprise of many experts, and although this trend cannot continue indefinitely for physical reasons, the immediate future will see further startling increases in computing speed. Increases in network capacity (also known as bandwidth) have also been huge, but rather less linear and predictable than increases in power because there are different factors that come into play here. Bandwidth is delivered through copper wiring which has a relatively low capacity, through optical fibre cables, which have almost infinite capacity, and through wireless transmission, which has variable capacity, given that portions of the airwaves have to be assigned with care to avoid interference of signals.

Adding bandwidth can mean a process of digging up roads and laying cables to replace earlier wiring, a hugely expensive procedure, which must be funded by many different commercial and public bodies in most countries.

Storage capabilities for digital data have also been growing exponentially: in the mid-1980s a 20Mb hard drive was regarded as massive storage, and 256Kb of RAM as sufficient memory. Now even laptop computers come supplied with 20Gb hard drives and 256Mb of RAM, which is 1000 times the capacity of machines of less than 20 years ago. But we need all this power and capacity to deal with the data that is coming our way in many media formats, as digital text, digital images, digital video and digital sound.

An average page of digital text takes around 20Kb of storage space, which means that there can be 32,500 pages stored on an average 650Mb CD-ROM. High-quality professional digital cameras and scanners can potentially capture digital reproductions of the original in such detail as to require at least 300Mb of storage space, allowing just two images to be stored on an average CD-ROM, and moving images and sound are even more hungry of space and power, though there are advantages in data compression that are helping to reduce the load. Data compression comes in two forms: 'lossless', which means that the compressed file loses no information in the compression and decompression processes, and 'lossy', where there is data loss in the processes.

Lossy compression gives more compact results than lossless, resulting in smaller files to store or transport, but the derived images are of a lower quality—which may not matter if the files are for web delivery, but which is unacceptable for high-quality printing or long-term storage. Increase of capacity and power in any of the component areas of digital processing and transmission are not just linear benefits: the relationship between demand and supply is complex and paradoxical. For example, a desktop computer would probably give excellent service for eight to ten years, but is likely to be replaced in most professional or even personal environments in two to four years. The resale value is likely to be very low, if there is any value left in the machine at all. This is because new developments render hardware and software obsolete so rapidly. Compare this with other everyday machinery, the car for instance.

There are people who change their cars every couple of years, for a variety of reasons to do with reliability, economy or prestige, but rarely because a particular model has become obsolete and will not run on certain roads, and there is certainly considerable resale value left in most cars. In the world of information supply, it is difficult to know whether the advances are driven by user demand or by the commercial imperatives of the suppliers of information and the suppliers of technology. Libraries are caught in the middle, having to purchase and provide ever more expensive and technologically demanding content to a wider range of users across a greater demographic and geographic area.

Creation of Digital Data

Despite the difficulties of the early technology, some scholars recognised the value of the computational manipulation of textual materials immediately. Text had to be painstakingly entered on punched cards or tape, but the benefits appeared so great in terms of retrieval and analysis that they persisted. Father Roberto Busa, for instance, formulated the idea of automated linguistic analysis of text in the years 1942-6, and started working with IBM in New York in 1947. He produced more than six million punched cards for his edition of the works of Thomas Aquinas, and in 1992 the first edition of his CD-ROM was published.

In the 1980s a new technology appeared in the form of the Kurzweil Data Entry Machine (KDEM), which was developed to provide texts for the blind. It used optical character recognition (OCR) to create electronic text for printing on Braille printers or (eventually) conversion to sound using text-to-speech processing. The KDEM was extremely expensive (in the tens of thousands of dollars), but it could be trained to recognise different typefaces and fonts, and it was relatively accurate—probably as accurate as modern OCR packages. Other text conversion needs could, of course, be satisfied using the KDEM, and large corpora of digital text were created for many purposes.

Digital text is now everywhere, as output from word-processors, publishers and OCR engines. Interestingly, OCR is faster and cheaper than it was in the 1980s, but it is still not as accurate as it needs to be to replace rekeying and typesetting, especially if the materials are pre-20th century. Many library projects use OCR to capture bodies of printed text; others, where the text is too difficult or a higher level of accuracy is needed, use rekeying. However, there are some new developments in the processing of text that greatly improve retrieval from inaccurate OCR. For maximum usefulness, digital text needs more than representations of alphanumeric symbols on the printed page; it also needs metadata to record other information about the textual object from which it derived.

Markup languages such as the Standard Generalised Markup Language (SGML), define textual metadata and specify complex schemas of standard metadata tags to inform all the processes to which digital text might be subject: description, retrieval, preservation, print output, and so on. While early document-processing technologies generally operated on strings of linear text, the possibilities of hypertextual linking within documents were recognised too, though this was initially difficult to implement on a computer.

Despite the claims of many modern gurus of cybernetic hypertext theory, written text is not linear but can be interlinked, interwoven and annotated on the printed page in highly complex structures not susceptible of computational representation by the first generations of hardware and software. From the mid-1980s, better screen technology, more processing power, the development of the mouse and the advent of the Graphical User Interface (GUI) have transformed the ability of the computer to represent and link documentary objects.

In the last five years, digital camera technology has developed to the extent that digital images can be captured that equal or even exceed largeformat analogue photographic reproductions. These have disadvantages, however: the cameras are expensive, and the file sizes huge, which causes problems for storage and delivery. However, from valuable originals, large archive images can be captured and stored for the long term, with lowerquality derivatives being delivered for viewing and printing. This is acceptable for most uses, and means that good-quality images can be integrated with other media for a more complete user experience. High-quality sound reproduction accompanies the images, allowing users to hear the religious offices that make up the text being sung by a monastic choir.

Now documents can be represented by high-quality images, with underlying searchable text, and with annotations in text, sound or video. Cameras are being developed that can capture 3-D images, and there are sophisticated capture devices for digital sound and video, deriving in part from the huge growth in these formats in the entertainment industry. It is, of course, possible to treat the printed page as an image. Capturing digital images from printed pages has the advantage that the page will appear on the screen exactly as it was in the original. The disadvantage of this presentation is that the search and retrieval functions are lost, but a combination of both image and text representation means that documents can be represented by images, with underlying searchable text and with annotations.

There is a rhetoric that suggests that we are moving rapidly from print to digital media: this is not borne out by evidence from the publishing industry and from copyright libraries. The death of the book has been predicted with every new communication or entertainment technology, the telegraph, recorded speech, film, television and the internet, but the book seems to be thriving. At the beginning of the 21st century, the UK copyright libraries, for instance, are receiving more print material than ever before, and this is without the materials that they purchase. Production of digital data is certainly on the increase, but it does not seem to be accompanied by a concomitant diminution in the printed output, though it is changing both the publishing industry and the world of libraries.

In the 15th century, the introduction of the printing press industrialised the production of books, but did not do away with handwriting. What it did do was change book production from a cottage industry carried out in monasteries to a commercial industry, and incidentally resulted in a huge loss of authority on the part of the Christian Church in Europe. Early printing presses were wooden and were hand-operated, and the type was hand-set. This remained the case until the beginning of the 19th century, when things changed rapidly with one of those 'paradigm shifts'.

Printing-press technology moved to iron presses, operated by steam, to mechanical type, to hotmetal type to phototypesetting and then to computer typesetting by the 1970s. Publishing began to become a separate industry from printing in the 18th century, and grew rapidly throughout the 19th century with the increasing mechanisation of the processes, and the further growth of literacy rates and the demands of a reading public. 'The total book production of the nineteenth century exceeded that of the eighteenth by 440%', and many of the publishing giants that still control the industry (though in very different configurations) came into being during this period.

Computer typesetting brought an unanticipated by-product: electronic text. This was not always kept initially, and when it was, the typesetting codes used for marking up the text rendered it largely unusable for any other process. However, standardisation of markup languages has meant that it is now possible to use electronic text for purposes other than printing, and many publishers have embraced electronic publishing in the last five years, especially in the production of journals. With the revolution in printing and the birth of the publishing industry came new developments in libraries.

In the Middle Ages in Europe, libraries were either monastic institutions holding relatively few, very valuable books or belonged to private individuals. Many of the great libraries of today are based upon some of the collections of these monasteries and individuals. When the British army invaded the city of Washington in 1814 and burned the Capitol, including the 3000-volume Library of Congress, Thomas Jefferson sold his personal library to the Congress to 'recommence' its library. The purchase of Jefferson's 6487 volumes for $23,940 was approved in 1815.

In the 18th century, circulation libraries and subscription libraries started to appear to satisfy the demands of the larger reading public for cheap access to print, and the 19th century saw the rise of the great public libraries. Librarians have always sought to mechanise routine processes as much as possible, and so were early adopters of computer technologies. Database programs were developed early in the history of computing for use in stock control, payroll systems and other commercial activities. The adoption of administrative systems for catalogue record creation was an early example of the use of computerised processes in libraries. This started as merely a means of producing, for manual filing, printed catalogue cards or slips, which would be referred to by library staff and users as a means of finding library resources.

To extend the duplication of catalogues and thus the number of user access points to the catalogue, microformats were used, 'enabling multiple copies of the catalogue to be distributed for the first time and new sequences, such as title catalogues, to be introduced'. Alongside this new capability to share catalogues, there started co-operative efforts to share the cataloguing load and to benefit from aggregating cataloguing effort across multiple libraries. Because bibliographic description is such a highly structured construct, the computerisation of the catalogue was a significant and inevitable next step from these early mechanisation initiatives. This was not the computerised catalogue as we know it now in the guise of the OPAC (Online Public Access Catalogue), but a straightforward listing of the library's resources with no links to borrower records or to external resources.

In tandem with the development of the computerised catalogue came the move to automate circulation functions. Initially, this was no more than associating a borrower number with a book accession number while the full records of each were kept on separate computer database or paper systems. Even these most basic functions were only available to the largest libraries because of the great expense involved. However, this was to change as computing technology became more widespread and software developed the capability to create connections between different parts of databases and to integrate functions in a primitive fashion. As soon as it was possible to get the circulation system to 'talk' to the catalogue, it was possible to automate some library functions, such as overdue notices.

As important as the mechanisation of routine staff-intensive functions, was the means it gave library managers to measure and assess borrower activity in great detail for the first time through reports generated from the computer logs and databases. This knowledge greatly enhanced acquisitions and stock management strategies and has helped librarians to cope proactively with changes in funding structures, borrower requirements and the user community, and with the accelerating expansion in information resources.

Computing

At the start of the 1980s, automated library functions were generally being achieved through mainframe computers with dumb terminals in large institutions, and it was not until the spread of personal computing that computerisation could be seriously afforded by small libraries such as those in schools, smaller businesses, hospitals or other small specialised organisations. The concentration of computer activity in one central processing point also limited those libraries with geographically distant outstations such as public libraries or large universities, and often the computing resources could only be made available in the main library location.

It was only with the inception of personal computers, local- and wide-area networks, and the movement from centralised to distributed client-server processing that libraries of all types were able to utilise fully the power of computing technology to automate functions, share information and resources, generate management reports and electronically link libraries together. From the perspective of the library user, they were experiencing computers in the library for the first time not as something which librarians used to facilitate library management, but as a direct point of service to use independently of the library staff.

By the early 1990s, almost all library functions were supported by automation in some way. Functions such as cataloguing, acquisitions, journals, circulation, interlibrary loans, financial control, stock management and user details were all integrated and automated to some extent. This period also saw a large growth in the electronic communication of data from one library to another. Librarians had for many years accessed remote database services for access to reference information and bibliographic data, using a dial-up connection to a local computer which would route information to the host machine, possibly based somewhere else in Europe or America. This was an early form of internetwork access, charging heavy fees not just on connect time, but on a per-item-retrieved basis.

In most libraries the end-user could not be given direct access because of the high cost of use (with legal and pharmaceutical-based libraries sometimes the exception) and the librarian was required as a skilled intermediary, and also as a buffer against over-expenditure. As wide-area networks in the USA, UK and elsewhere developed, the emphasis on connect time was relaxed as annual subscriptions with unlimited access were introduced by suppliers. CD-ROM versions of databases for personal computers also relaxed the need to limit end-user access.

Wider use of networking enabled libraries to share more data in the form of interlibrary loans, electronic document delivery, electronic mail and also electronic ordering functions, also known as EDI or Electronic Data Interchange.

Electronic Data Interchange (EDI) refers to the computer exchange of business information using a standardised data format. Standardised EDI messages are based on common business documents such as purchase orders, invoices and delivery notes, which are interchanged between computer systems without human intervention or interpretation. It has been in use since the 1970s, but it was not until the late 1980s and early 1990s that any attempt was made to move away from proprietary systems to open standards.

Adopting EDI can eliminate the mailing of paper documentation and the manual processing of quotations, purchase orders, invoices, shipping documents, customs documents, and other business transactions. Because the data is processed and stored automatically, tasks such as re-keying data and printing purchase orders and invoices are eliminated. The use of EDI has been as significant a development for libraries as for the business world.

The integration of the cataloguing and ordering process, plus the ability to chase orders that have not arrived on time automatically, speeds up acquisitions and gets resources to the user more quickly on their arrival. Automated financial controls can be pre-set to generate purchase orders and fiscal reports, and also to limit certain types of expenditure to defined budgetary plans. Librarians, as early adopters of EDI, have been among the first to partake in e-commerce and thus understand e-commerce's trials and tribulations but also its great advantages to the management of library services.

As far back as 1902 we can trace how basic technology was used and the results shared by libraries in a co-operative way. In that year the Library of Congress began selling printed cards that in effect 'made that library the centralised cataloguing agency for thousands of American libraries'. In computing terms we have to wait until 1971 for the same level of resource sharing and economy, when OCLC introduced an online shared cataloguing system for libraries.

Today this co-operative catalogue is available to libraries in 76 countries and territories around the world, with over 46 million cataloguing records available, as well as associated interlibrary loan and reference database services. In the UK, the Birmingham Libraries Co-operative Mechanisation Project (BLCMP) was established in 1969 as a joint venture between libraries in Birmingham. BLCMP was created to realise the benefits of a shared approach to library computing and built a large shared database of over 19 million bibliographic records.

The Research Libraries Group (RLG) also provides extensive shared resources through a set of online catalogues that offer millions of records describing materials created around the world. In many areas, libraries are showing intensive co-operation and sharing of the fruits of computing technology. NORDINFO (the Nordic Council for Scientific Information), which celebrated its 25th anniversary in 2001, was founded as a bridge between Nordic research libraries and the growing information and documentation sector. The general objective set for the coming years is to work towards what has been called 'The Nordic Electronic Research Library'. Another significant example of sharing for mutual benefit is the important realm of interlibrary loans.

No single library holds all published information and most cannot hold even a sizeable sliver of it, but the librarian's role is clearly to provide access to the complete body. The only sensible solution is to share access to the resources through interlibrary loan. All the above co-operatives support this and local cooperatives for interlending exist all over the world at regional and national levels. Most of this is now being managed or documents delivered via electronic means. The British Library Document Supply Centre, for instance, received 34% of requests by postal means in 1993-4 but now receives less than 13% by post and the remainder by electronic means.

Online Libraries

Every library is different, every digital library is different, and different players are advancing many definitions for the digital library. Arms, for instance, defines a digital library as: a managed collection of information, with associated services, where the information is stored in digital formats and accessible over a network. A crucial part of this definition is that the information is managed. For the Digital Library Federation in the USA: Digital libraries are organisations that provide the resources, including the specialised staff, to select, structure, offer intellectual access to, interpret, distribute, preserve the integrity of, and ensure the persistence over time of collections of digital works so that they are readily and economically available for use by a defined community or set of communities.

Some prefer to work with the concept of the 'hybrid' library, as they believe that this more closely describes the reality of libraries, which have always been hybrid. The digital is one more (albeit very different) format that librarians have to deal with in a multi-format environment, where for many years non-documentary mixed-media objects, both analogue and digital, have been growing in importance, and where technology for access has had to be provided. Most libraries can supply microfilm and microfiche readers, video players, audio tape and CD players, as well as terminals for access to digital resources.

However, there are often strategic reasons for defining activities as coming under a digital libraries heading—the possibility of securing funding, for instance, from programmes which are defined as digital library initiatives. Hybrid libraries are designed to bring a range of technologies from different sources together in the context of a working library, and also to begin to explore integrated systems and services in both the electronic and print environments. They exist 'on the continuum between the conventional and digital library, where electronic and paper-based information sources are used alongside each other'.

The concepts of virtual libraries or libraries without walls reflect the integrative possibilities inherent in the digital: if significant library collections are digital, then the confines of space no longer define boundaries upon information. Virtual collections from many different sources can be assembled and accessed from anywhere, without the user even knowing where the sources reside, and personal virtual collections can be built to serve many purposes. Hence a virtual library could potentially be enormous, linking huge collections from all around the world together, or it could be very small, being the personal digital collection of one individual.

Digital libraries are, like any so-called revolutionary change, a development of a whole range of underlying theories and technologies that have come together to create a paradigm shift. The speed of recent developments has taken some librarians by surprise, especially the exponential growth of the amount of digital data available, but they are understandable if we look at some of the precursors that have led to the current trends: new developments rarely spring fully formed from the ether. There are many different kinds of digital libraries creating, delivering and preserving digital objects that derive from many different formats of underlying data, and it is very difficult to formulate a definition that encapsulates all these.

5

Modern Media and Social Issues

Media stereotypes are inevitable, which need as wide an audience as possible to quickly understand information. Aboriginal people have been vigorously stereotyped in words and images for hundreds of years. Film, television and comic-book producers have perpetuated these stereotypes over several generations, and so old notions of what it is to be a Canadian Aboriginal or a Native American have lived on well past the emergence of a public consciousness that knows better.

For over a hundred years, Westerns and documentaries have shaped the public's perception of Native people. The wise elder (Little Big Man); the drunk (Tom Sawyer); the Indian princess (Pocahontas); the loyal sidekick (Tonto)-these images have become engrained in the consciousness of every North American. Hollywood's versions of "how the West was won" relied totally on the presence of Native tribes, who were to be wiped out or reined in. "And, for the longest time," says Canadian Ojibway playwright Drew Hayden Taylor, "there wasn't a real 'Indian' to be seen on the movie sets: Native 'representation' was taken care of by Italians or Spaniards-anyone with dark enough skin to save on makeup."

As the portrayals of Native characters-either as primitive, violent and deceptive or else as passive and full of childlike obedience-extended to TV, novels and comics, they became familiar, comfortable signposts for much of Western civilisation whenever it needed to acknowledge the Aboriginal presence. Since few people, especially in larger urban centres, actually came into contact with Indigenous populations, these portrayals, however inaccurate, had all the more impact. Though popular U.S. films rarely looked north of the border, these stereotypes etched themselves just as deeply into the Canadian psyche. "We were well into the second half of the 20th century before it occurred to filmmakers that Native people were still around, and even leading interesting lives," says Taylor.

Television in the United States has been slower to respond to criticism. Indigenous faces are still almost entirely absent from the small screen, except in the news or in documentaries. There have been a few efforts to change the situation, however. In the late 1990s, the American Indian Registry for the Performing Arts in Los Angeles published a directory of Native American performing arts professionals. And in 2001, after acknowledging that "Native Americans are virtually invisible on TV," CBS and NBC held talent showcases in major cities across North America to strengthen their databases of Aboriginal performers. The new climate of "political correctness" has combined with genuine effort to counter some of the more overt forms of racism in films and television-but subtle vestiges of Native stereotyping still remain. Some of the most common stereotyping traps are various forms of romanticisation; historical inaccuracies; stereotyping by omission; and simplistic characterisations.

Farmer cites the successful Canadian film Black Robe, about a Jesuit missionary's quest to save the Huron's souls, as typical of the one-sided historical accounts that upset Aboriginal people. "Black Robe misses a key element," says Farmer. "Nobody explains the Iroquois Confederacy's five centuries of peace between the six nations. The Hurons saw the devastation from the alcohol brought by the newcomers as a decay that had to be rooted out. The Iroquois told the Hurons that everyone not affected should leave, and they would go in and clean the area out."

Farmer contends that there's never been an understanding of why that was done-and so the story of a classic conflict between Indigenous and non-Indigenous peoples has never been told. All vestiges of truth-and thereby of intercultural understanding-give way here before the onslaught of movieland's mythic creation. Film and TV producers have never let details get in the way of a good story. Nowhere is this more true than in depictions of Aboriginal life, where artistic license is liberally taken in portraying dress, customs, livelihoods and spiritual beliefs and ceremonies.

This reduction of cultural heritage and diversity (which most audiences do not even notice) is seen by critics as both a symptom of the problem (not taking Aboriginal people seriously) and an unconscious yet systematic way of perpetuating erroneous stereotypes. What occurs in many films, says social critic Ward Churchill, "is roughly parallel to having a Catholic priest wear a Rabbi's headgear and Protestant cleric's garb while conducting High Mass before a Satanist pentagram, simply because each of these disparate physical manifestations of spiritual culture is visually interesting in its own right."

Most film depictions of Native people are set in a 50-year period in the mid-19th century. Where were Native

North Americans before the coming of the white man, and where are they now? Apparently "Indians" did not survive the transition to modern society. The most flagrant omission in movies and television is the Aboriginal woman. When she is included, it is most often as a "sexual savage" (who cannot be tamed and must therefore be degraded and eventually conquered).

Perhaps most destructive to the image of Aboriginal people is the lack of character and personality accorded them by the media. Aboriginal people are almost always cast in supporting roles or relegated to the background, and are rarely allowed to speak or display a real personality. And what character they do have tends to reveal itself only in terms of their interactions with white people. Rarely is an Aboriginal portrayed as having personal strengths and weaknesses, or shown acting on his or her own values and judgements. Nor is the Native ever allowed to tell his or her own story. Most stories are conveyed through the lens of the European experience.

A common device used by Hollywood to attach familiar values to Native acts has been to script a white character as narrator (Dances with Wolves, Thunderheart). While this purports to treat the American Indian sympathetically, the reality is that the Aboriginal is robbed of voice. A number of academics contend Hollywood's depictions of Aboriginal people are based on much broader motives than simply winning audiences.

Many of the myths and misperceptions that persist among non-Aboriginal people are perpetuated by no communication, poor communication or one-sided communication. It often seems that the only coverage Native people receive in the news media centres on political and constitutional issues, forest fires, poverty and substance or sexual abuse. Occasionally, stories about cultural activities appear on some local stations-but these are usually given only passing mention. And when it comes to issues that affect all Canadians, Aboriginal people are rarely, if ever, consulted. Of course, the fundamental nature of news and news reporting is that the bad news gets all the attention.

Tragedies, conflicts and crises get reported; success stories rarely do. But the end result is that a non-Native audience may well come to the conclusion that Aboriginal people are a troubled, plagued and contentious people. Rudy Platiel, who spent 27 years covering the Aboriginal beat for the Globe and Mail, notes that, "There are an awful lot of good things happening that are not going to get reported in the mainstream press unless somebody pushes to get them there." The mainstream media owe it to their communities to reflect the cities, towns and rural areas by making their newsrooms as diverse as their communities. There are a number of causes for poor reporting on Aboriginal issues.

Journalists have tight deadlines and are rarely given adequate time to thoroughly investigate issues; the gatekeepers of newsrooms and newspapers are seldomwell-versed in Aboriginal affairs; and there is a dearth of experienced Aboriginal journalists. Aboriginal people make up over three per cent of the Canadian population. But in a 1994 study by the Diversity Committee of the Canadian Newspaper Association, of the 41 mainstream papers surveyed (employing 2,620 reporters, copy editors, photographers and supervisors) only four people were Aboriginal. These factors all contribute to the perpetuation of incomplete and, in some cases, biased information.

Over the years, for example, much coverage has been given to the "tax-free" status of Canadian Aboriginals-

leaving many Canadians to believe that all Native people share a lucrative tax-exempt status. What is less well known is that only those working on reserves are eligible, and the unemployment rate in these communities is high since opportunities for work are quite limited.

For several decades now, media critics and feminists alike have been examining the role of the media in creating and reinforcing stereotypical representations of women and femininity. But only recently have they expanded the research to consider how the media also construct, inform and reinforce prevalent ideas about men and masculinity. Mainstream media representations also play a role in reinforcing ideas about what it means to be a "real" man in our society. In most media portrayals, male characters are rewarded for self-control and the control of others, aggression and violence, financial independence, and physical desirability. Various media analysts and researchers argue that media portrayals of male characters fall within a range of stereotypes.

Sports Media

Sports media also contribute to the construction of masculinity in contemporary society. A study conducted by the Amateur Athletic Foundation of Los Angeles reports that 98 per cent of American boys between the ages of 8 and 17 consume sports media. Since professional sports are virtually dominated by men-from the athletes and coaches to the commentators and reporters-sports media have the potential to transmit powerful ideas about manliness and masculinity. Recent studies on gender and sports media find that sports commentary reinforces perceptions of "violent masculinity."

By praising athletes who continue to play while injured, and by using language of conflict and war to describe action, sports commentary reinforces violence and aggression as exciting and rewarding behaviour. Sports broadcasts focus heavily on violence in professional sports, often replaying and over-analysing footage of graphic injuries, accidents and fights.

Masculinity and Advertising

In its study of masculinity and sports media, the research group hildren Now in U.S, found that most commercials directed to male viewers tend to air during sports programming. Women rarely appear in these commercials, and when they do, they're generally portrayed in stereotypical ways. In fact, in his analysis of gender in advertising, author and University of North Texas professor Steve Craig argues that women tend to be presented as "rewards" for men who choose the right product. He describes such commercials as "narratives of playful escapades away from home and family." They operate, he says, at the level of fantasy-presenting idealised portrayals of men and women.

When he focused specifically on beer commercials, Craig found that the men were invariably "virile, slim and white"-and the women always "eager for male companionship." Author and academic Susan Bordo (University of Kentucky) has also analysed gender in advertising, and agrees that men are usually portrayed as virile, muscular and powerful. Their powerful bodies dominate space in the ads. For women, the focus is on slenderness, dieting, and attaining a feminine ideal; women are always presented as not just thin, but also weak and vulnerable. These critics and others suggest that just as traditional advertising has for decades sexually objectified women and their bodies, today's marketing campaigns are objectifying men in the same way.

A 2002 study by the University of Wisconsin suggests that this new focus on fit and muscled male bodies is causing men the same anxiety and personal insecurity that women have felt for decades. "Representation of the world, like the world itself, is the work of men; they describe it from their own point of view, which they confuse with the absolute truth." Non-white or working class men are also marginalised. Men who are members of minority groups are typically called upon as experts only in response to minority community matters, drugs and crime. And, as Barbara Ehrenreich notes, news and current affairs programming portrays working class men as dumb, inarticulate and old-fashioned.

Although information media are often presented as informed and "objective," many commentators argue that white male dominance of these media helps perpetuate sexism, racism, and class privilege in society. It is also argued that such coverage presents white masculinity as the social and cultural norm. Entertainment media reinforce the stereotypes of the rich white male and the working class buffoon. Richard Butsch argues that television programmes tend to exaggerate affluence, and portray working class men as immature, irresponsible, and requiring the supervision of their "betters."

Media educators Larry Gross and George Gerbner argue that the media participate in the "symbolic annihilation" of gays and lesbians by negatively stereotyping them (often consigning them to the margins of entertainment media, playing either "colourful" and "flamboyant" characters or dangerous psychopaths), by rarely portraying them realistically, or by not portraying them at all. Gross and Gerbner argue that the commercial structure of the mass media limits the opportunity for representing diverse characters. Too often networks and film companies shy away from portraying gays and lesbians for fear of alienating or offending advertisers, investors, and audiences. Any discussion of the portrayal of gays and lesbians on television must consider the commercial demands of the medium.

But in recent years there has been some improvement in the representation of gays and lesbians on mainstream network television. The popularity of shows such as Will & Grace, La vie, la vie... or Queer Eye for the Straight Guy illustrates that networks are willing to feature gay characters, as long as the shows draw high ratings, and generate profits for advertisers. This profit-motivation means that networks are careful in their portrayals of gay and lesbian characters. While Will & Grace does feature two openly gay male characters, there is little or no discussion about gay relationships or romance. The two gay characters are friends, not lovers, and are rarely shown in romantic situations.

The primary relationship for both gay men is with the heterosexual female characters. In fact, this seems to be an emerging trend. In the past few years, Hollywood has developed a new genre: the gay/straight romance. Television shows such as Will & Grace and films such as My Best Friend's Wedding, The Object of My Affection, and The Next Best Thing all portray a gay man and straight woman as the "perfect couple." While some critics have suggested that this trend represents an attempt to include gay and lesbian characters, others state that such representations still marginalise and silence the experiences of gays and lesbians.

Though mainstream television and movies continue to "sanitise" the portrayal of gay and lesbian life, speciality and pay-TV channels have begun to show more cutting-edge, controversial and critically acclaimed series about gays and lesbians. In 1999, for instance, Britain's Channel 4 made history when it broadcast a miniseries focusing on the lives and loves of three gay men living in Manchester. The series, called Queer as Folk, was highly rated not only by the gay community but also by the mainstream press. The series was not without controversy-some people complained that the subject matter was inappropriate and others were upset that one of the characters was only 15 years old.

Still others worried that it portrayed gay men as over-sexed. But despite these criticisms, the series also enjoyed international success; it aired on ShowCase, Canada's speciality channel and it also inspired an American version, which airs on Showtime. Many people see the success of Queer as Folk as evidence that "lesbigay" shows can still be enormously popular and profitable. However, advertisers and sponsors are cautious about affiliating themselves with such cutting-edge programming. When the American version of Queer as Folk was in production, fashion houses such as Versace, Prada, Polo Ralph Lauren and Abercrombie & Fitch refused to allow their brands to appear in the series. And although the show is set in Pittsburgh, the marketing director of the Pittsburgh Steelers wrote a letter to the producers demanding that all references to the team be removed.

"In a hundred years of movies, homosexuality has only rarely been depicted on the screen. When it did appear, it was there as something to laugh at-or something to pity-or even something to fear. These were fleeting images, but they were unforgettable, and they left a lasting legacy. Hollywood, that great maker of myths, taught straight people what to think about gay people ... and gay people what to think about themselves." Recent controversies over Hollywood's negative depiction of homosexuality have focused on how such portrayals marginalise and silence gays and lesbians.

Organisations such as the Gay and Lesbian Alliance Against Defamation (GLAAD) argue that films such as Basic Instinct and The Silence of the Lambs demonise gays and lesbians by portraying them as psychopaths. In his book *The Celluloid Closet*, Vito Russo analyses the representation of gays and lesbians in Hollywood films from the 1890s to the 1980s, and demonstrates a history of homophobia. He argues that Hollywood's portrayal of lesbians and gay men has often been cruel and homophobic. Gay and lesbian characters have been defined by their sexual orientation, and lacked any complex character development.

From the 1930s to the 1950s, religious and women's groups criticised Hollywood films for contributing to immorality. As a result, the industry introduced a self-censorship code that affected the portrayal of homosexuality. During these years, films could not feature overtly homosexual characters-so homosexuality was suggested through a character's mannerisms and behaviour. This strict code was loosened in the 1960s and 1970s, which also saw the dawn of the women's movement and the gay rights movement. While gays and lesbians were becoming more visible and vocal in public life, their representation in films was becoming even more homophobic. At this time, gay characters were often represented as dangerous, violent, or murderous.

Since the 1990s, Hollywood has improved its portrayal of gay and lesbian characters. The popularity of films such as The Birdcage, Philadelphia, To Wong Foo, Flawless and In & Out demonstrates that audiences can and do enjoy films with gay and lesbian characters. But despite these advances, critics say that the industry is still too cautious in its portrayals of gay themes, characters, and experiences. Hollywood films are designed to appeal to as large an audience as possible; and producers fear that focusing on gay and lesbian themes risks offending a large portion of the audience, as well as potential investors. While considerable progress has been made with respect to the depiction of gays and lesbians in television and movies, critics argue that news media still systematically ignore and distort the lives and experiences of gays and lesbians.

In a 1998 study that analysed 50 years of coverage of gay and lesbian issues in Time and Newsweek, Lisa Bennett found that news media reinforce prejudice and discrimination against gays and lesbians. She observes that gays and lesbians are often linked to deviant or criminal behaviour without evidence to support such claims; and that the media often reprint offensive and homophobic comments. Bennett concludes that such practices reinforce assumptions that gays and lesbians are inherently inferior.

Before the dawn of the gay rights movement in the 1970s, gays and lesbians did not figure prominently in mainstream news media. But with the emergence of HIV/AIDS as a public health issue in the 1980s, coverage became more intense, and more negative. During this time, media coverage often portrayed gay men as a serious risk to society. Activists and academics such as Simon Watney, Douglas Crimp and Jan Zita Grover argue that news coverage of HIV/AIDS has consistently drawn on negative stereotypes about gays and lesbians. In their view, the coverage of HIV/AIDS in the 1980s reflected mainstream society's fear of and dislike for the gay community-and essentially blamed gay men for AIDS.

The media coverage of HIV/AIDS improved in the 1990s, largely as a result of the efforts of activists fighting for gay and lesbian rights. But the mainstream media still tend to cover the gay community only when it is perceived to be in crisis. Many argue that, since gays and lesbians comprise approximately two to five per cent of the population, their interests and perspectives should be more readily addressed. Organisations such as the Gay and Lesbian Alliance Against Defamation (GLAAD) maintain that print, news and entertainment media do not adequately address or reflect gay experiences and perspectives.

Gays and lesbians tend to appear in the news or on television only when there is a specific issue that interests or directly affects the gay community. Participants at a 2000 Roundtable of Gays and Lesbians in Quebec came to the same conclusion, saying in their report that the lack of gay news items and the reduction of questions touching the gay and lesbian communities renders the presence of homosexuals in the news "occasional and marginal."

The media are making progress in its depiction of gays and lesbians. Perhaps the most striking example of this is the active courting of gay and lesbian consumers through gay-positive advertising and marketing campaigns. In 1994, IKEA aired a commercial that depicted two gay men shopping for a dining room set, making the store the first company to actively target gay consumers. Since that time, many companies have started to target gay and lesbian consumers with gay-positive marketing campaigns. These campaigns are directed to a specific market: gay men and lesbians who live in cities, are single and have a large amount of disposable income.

Impacts of Media on White People

"White people create the dominant images of the world, and don't quite see that they thus construct the world in their image." Discussions of media stereotyping have tended to focus on how traditionally marginalised groups such as women, gay men, lesbians, and ethnic minorities have been negatively affected by stereotypical portrayals. But increasingly, scholars are considering how stereotyping privileges certain groups.

Biology alone does not determine racial identity. The concept of race is equally shaped by social norms and expectations, which are based on historical events and current practices. In North American society, being white is perceived as the norm. Often the fact that whiteness is also a race is not acknowledged. As a result, researchers have begun to examine whiteness and to define it in terms of social impact. Such research concentrates on "white privilege"-the differences in power between whites and non-whites, and the advantages white people automatically take for granted. The advantages of being white include learning the history of one's own race in school, to seeing members of one's own ethnic group widely represented in the media, to being confident that job refusals are not based on one's race.

Most of the decision-makers in North American news and entertainment media are white. Media ownership is mainly concentrated in the hands of white males; white journalists dominate the mainstream media; and white people hold most creative positions in the entertainment media as actors, writers and directors. All these factors contribute to the prevalence of whiteness in media, and help to reinforce white privilege as the norm. Most mainstream media content also reinforces white privilege by featuring white characters and addressing white interests and experiences. When programming does feature non-white characters, they usually appear in supporting roles.

Social researchers and scholars point out that the mainstream media typically skew their portrayals of economic classes towards the white middle and upper classes, with all their privileges. They rarely represent the interests or perspectives of working-class women and men. Working wives in television series tend to be middle class women in pursuit of careers. Depictions of working class wives are rare. Working-class men tend to be shown as immature, irresponsible, and requiring the supervision of their "betters."

Impact of Stereotyping

Generations of North American children have grown up watching "cowboys and Indians" films and TV shows and reading books such as The Adventures of Tom Sawyer and Little House on the Prairie. Popular films and novels reinforced the notion that Aboriginal people existed only in the past-forever chasing buffalo or being chased by the cavalry. These images showed them as forever destined to remain on the margins of "real" society. Such impressions and childhood beliefs, set at an early age, are often the hardest to shake. While the old-style Westerns are long gone, today's media producers still continue their tradition.

For instance, Disney's Peter Pan may be a new take on an old tale, but its stereotyping of Indians as cruel and malicious, with their articulation reduced to "ugh" and their dress to loincloths, is as strong as ever. The same can be said for Pocahontas even though that film was more politically correct. How can a child negotiate the distance between portrayals like these, and "real" First Nations people?

Anyone who understands or studies the social development of children and young people knows that attitudes, values and self-esteem are well developed by the mid-teen years, or even earlier. What young people see and hear in the media helps them to figure out how the world works and who and what is valued in our society. If the media's take on Aboriginal people is interpreted at face value, then kids are growing up with a skewed vision of what it means to be part of a First Peoples society. If they get their impressions from the news, they'll likely view Aboriginal people as a negative force. And if their impressions come from films and TV programmes, they'll learn to think of Aboriginal people as inferior (passive, aggressive or drunk) or simply as non-entities, obliterated by omission.

When young Aboriginal people read the newspaper or turn on the TV, how often do they see their own life experiences reflected? Almost never, says Children Now, the U.S. research organisation that analysed the presence of Native American children on TV in 1999, and conducted focus groups with children from 20 tribes. Furthermore, they contend, those children have learned to associate positive attributes with white television characters, and negative attributes with non-white characters. "The media have a lot of power to endorse stereotypes," says Susan Swan, an Ojibway from the Lake Manitoba First Nation. "We go into First Nations communities to talk to youth about gangs. When asked, the kids estimate that about 95 per cent of Aboriginal youth is involved in gangs. The actual number is three per cent. Why do they think these numbers are so high? It's because this is what they get from television and newspapers."

The popular media are "cool" in the eyes of most kids. If the existence and value of a group of people is not affirmed by inclusion in media information and entertainment, the message is clear-they're not important. In Aboriginal communities, this can contribute to, as one community sociologist calls it, "learned helplessness, alienation, and a sense of having no control." In Canada, new sensitivities and support for cultural diversity have brought some positive changes.

Aboriginal children are periodically featured or interviewed in children's after-school television; the National Film Board has made films for years that document real Aboriginal lives; the CBC has had many seasons of successful dramas that focus on Aboriginal communities; and Aboriginal entertainers have been "going mainstream" for two decades. These measures, along with the establishment of Aboriginal television and radio networks, all contribute to a more balanced view and more diverse voices.

Practically speaking, though, these voices still represent only a small proportion of the popular media that kids consume today. The evening news, the "Indian" images in sports-culture hype, the products of the Disney empire, and the misrepresentation (and non-representation) of Aboriginal people in most mainstream media-all continue to influence kids' views of Aboriginal cultures and peoples.

MEDIA EDUCATION

Media education can help young people put current images and messages about Aboriginal people into perspective by helping them understand how the media work, why stereotyping exists, how decisions are made, and why "it matters who makes it." Media education is not about learning the right answers; it's about consuming media images with an active, critical mind and asking the right questions. The following are the kinds of inquiries that can help to raise awareness about the portrayal of Aboriginal people in movies, television entertainment and current affairs programming.

Media education is that nothing is objective-each and every media production is created with a viewpoint and for a purpose. The "reality" depicted in film or television productions is the result of many choices and each of these choices is based on the experience, knowledge and bias of the producers involved. To date, very few films and TV shows featuring Aboriginal people have been written or produced by Aboriginal people-and it shows. The ownership of a TV station or newspaper, the makeup of its management team and its political leanings will all have an impact on who is interviewed on a current affairs programme, which "experts" are chosen for sound bites on an issue, and whose perspectives are ignored completely. When Aboriginal voices are heard, it's almost always on Aboriginal issues and rarely on general topics affecting society as a whole. A groundbreaking land treaty may get much less coverage than a group of Aboriginal people setting up a blockade.

Blockades and the potential for violence have visual appeal for television; men and women negotiating around a table don't. Likewise for sensational stories on murders, prostitution and drug abuse; they keep the ratings up, and high ratings mean good advertising revenues. Newscasts have to move along quickly and stereotyping is a kind of shorthand that people can comprehend without explanation. Understanding how the news works isn't going to change the news, but it does help kids understand that "newsworthy" stories are not necessarily the most important stories.

Comparing the news coverage of APTN (Aboriginal Peoples Television Network) with that of a national television network provides a strong lesson in media voices and behind-the-scenes decision-making. Are Aboriginal people shown as real human beings in films and TV programmes or do they seem wooden and two-dimensional? Media producers, especially those in Hollywood, have used Native people to tell white people's stories for generations. Rarely are Native characters given complex personalities or autonomous roles. Rarely do they rely on their own values and judgements, or act upon their own motivations. Although efforts have been made to undo this tradition, old stereotypes die hard.

Anyone with knowledge of the various Aboriginal cultures will pick out outrageous and often amusing inaccuracies-tipis where longhouses were used, horses where foot-and-canoe travel was the norm, feather headdresses on the Pacific coast. Distinctions in dress, language, abodes and beliefs of the many Aboriginal cultures are often ignored in favour of a shorthand that "speaks" to the audience. This may be due to laziness, ignorance or the desire to use visual props that will be recognised by audiences and visually arresting onscreen. A convenient convention of the old Westerns was to have Native people speaking in broken English, their thoughts and emotions restricted to their limited knowledge of English (and, it was usually implied, to their limited intellect). This tendency toward simplification has extended in some degree to modern-day characterisations of Aboriginal people.

If set in the past, the script should at least show Aboriginal characters speaking fluently in their own languages. There are over 350 different North American Aboriginal languages-a fact unacknowledged by the film industry. With few exceptions, Hollywood seems to have thought so. Native tribes flourished for thousands of years before the coming of Europeans and today there are over a million Canadian Aboriginal people and nearly two million Native Americans-some on reserves and others in rural and urban communities.

The development of information and communication media generating a digital cultured teens, emerging as tomorrow's youth. Teen sex is a major public health problem. The physical, emotional, and social consequences of teen sexual activity include high rates of teen pregnancy, and sexually transmitted diseases including AIDS. Each year 25% of sexually active teenagers contract a sexually transmitted disease (STD), and the younger a female is when she first has sex, the more likely it is that she will have "involuntary or forced" sex.

Many health professionals believe that mass media content depicting casual sex with no consequences has resulted in a host of negative behaviours among teens who may be persuaded that teen sexual activity is both acceptable and wide spread. Pediatric healthcare providers are being encouraged to assess patients' media use because of its potential association with unhealthy behaviours. Although parents and educators try to promote abstinence or condom use, teens are increasingly exposed to media sexual content that does not provide information about health risks and personal responsibility.

Both negative and positive advertising messages have been shown to influence young people, according to a pediatric medical association that calls on the mass media to promote responsible sex, and healthy behaviours. In addition to modelling unhealthy sexual behaviours, entertainment may negatively influence other aspects of teens' physical and psychological well-being. Research suggests that media portrayals of unrealistic body images negatively impact teens' self-esteem. Teens, especially young females, become discontent with their bodies and may develop unhealthy eating behaviours in an attempt to achieve media-ideal body types. Although family and social relationships also have an influence, teens learn about society and sexual relationships from visual media images portraying body types, clothing, and other cultural norms.

Sexual content in mass media has a profound real-life effect according to researchers who point to the co-evolution of media messages and sexual culture in American society. Mass media can either reinforce norms or offer insights into alternative ways of thinking. Entertainment content depicting sexual norms, stereotypes, double-standards, and sexual roles may have a profound influence on teens' perceptions about sex, body image, and social norms. Teens often seek social and sexual information from mass media sources rather than their parents or other adults. These teens may be attracted to programmes with sexual content.

In a study of prime-time television shows popular among young viewers, sexual references accounted for as much as 50% of character interactions. These programmes typically depicted sex as a "recreational" pursuit rather than something pertaining to relationships or reproduction, and the sexual content reinforced gender stereotypes of men as aggressors, and women as sexual objects who are valued for their physical appearances.

According to some studies, research implies that: teens who watch sexual content on television are more likely to engage in sex; teens who watch a lot of television tend to have negative attitudes about being a virgin; and teens who see sexual content as being more real are more impacted by the sexual content. Age and gender may also influence how teens select media, according to one study that found older teens were more likely to tune in to sexual content, and that females were more likely to learn about sex and relationships from sexual content in the media.

Music Television (MTV) is another example of electronic media programming that barrages teens with sexual messages. From the beginning, MTV transformed music into television programming by using fast-paced visuals to grab the attention of a very specific youthful audience—a new generation that had been raised with television and had different ways of processing information. In order to make the aural and visual elements fit together, music video producers and directors, rather than entertainers and writers, control visual images that may have nothing to do with the musicians' or artists' original concepts.

MTV became a programmer's dream of nonstop commercial television that changed the way people hear popular music and how they see the meanings that are embedded in the music content. Teens report that they watch MTV because it helps them to understand the songs better, and to understand what the music is about. However, the content that the teens are tuning into is more than 75% sexual, with stereotypical portrayals of males and females. MTV uses sexual images of women through "short, sharp, shots of intense visual pleasure" to encourage viewers to watch closely and stay focused so that they do not miss anything.

Camera angles and other production techniques in MTV videos depict women in violent scenes and women giving ambiguous yes/no signals. Visual images in videos are sexual even when the lyrics are not, according to researchers who say that "sex sells, in music videos and elsewhere". Some media effects researchers believe MTV sexual content influences how viewers perceive sex and sexual behaviours in society. Music videos that depict gender stereotypes and recreational sex without consequences influence teens' identity formation by modelling the world through these images.

A startling view of how entertainment content may influence sexual attitudes comes from a review of the 1984 US Attorney General's Commission on Pornography.

According to two researchers, whose studies were "cited throughout the two-volume work," the large government study condemned pornography, but failed to reveal that violent content, rather than explicit sexual content, was shown to have a greater impact on adult males' attitudes toward rape and sexual aggression. In controlled studies, males who were shown pornographic sex without violence had more negative attitudes toward rape than males who were shown violence without sex. These findings directly relate to teens, and others, who typically watch television and non-X-rated movies.

The prevalence of violence—even without sex—in mass media entertainment, according to the researchers, can contribute to more sexually aggressive attitudes among viewers. Despite myriad concerns over entertainment's influence on teens, some researchers argue that there is insufficient evidence of a causal relationship. They assert that studies demonstrating a correlation between sexual content in entertainment and teen sexual behaviours do not prove whether sexually active teens watch more sex or whether watching more sex encourages teens to be sexually active.

These researchers take a broader perspective of media influence on teen sexual culture, going beyond content and effects, to see how individual characteristics of ethnicity, gender, developmental stage, and socio-economic class influence teens' media use and the incorporation of media ideas into teens' daily lives. These researchers situate media influence on teen sexuality in the context of family, friends, school and other social situations that provide information and influence teens' sexual perceptions.

For example, early sexual experience is associated with lack of parental involvement, and beliefs that other teens are sexually active, while mitigating factors include parental involvement and teen participation in social activities that do not provide sexual opportunities. This interactive association is further influenced by individual predictive factors such as onset of physical maturity. According to these researchers, teens select and use media messages either to socially reproduce media images by following the status quo, or to socially resist media images by finding and following examples of alternative behaviour.

While many parents, educators, activists, and health professionals are working on solutions based on the perception that media sexual content influences teen audiences, researchers who view media influence in this complicated, contextualised perspective call for long-term media use studies to determine the actual influence of media on teen sexual culture. Academic researchers provide multiple perspectives, theories, and data that contribute to this media influence debate, sometimes facilitating progress, and sometimes the opposite.

Multiple academic disciplines including cultural studies, mass communications, communication science, psychology, linguistics, and English contribute to media influence research. These disciplines draw on various educational philosophies and myriad other political and social ideologies that inform research on message effects, content analysis, semiotics, audience analysis, and audience practice. Some researchers in the field of psychology argue that the mass media have a strong influence on audiences.

From psychological processes perspectives, "the media are instrumental in developing the constructs that are available in memory, and in determining which of those constructs are chronically accessible". According to some psychology researchers, this concept of construct accessibility helps to explain the media process because ideas work on "associations in memory" and media messages influence the basic constructs that impact how viewers see their social world and society. These researchers explain that construct accessibility might cause viewers who have seen a negative portrayal of police in recent entertainment to have a negative image of a recent real-life police incident.

Researchers explain that the concept of message context is the reason why advertisers do not place commercials next to news stories that might cause unfavourable associations with the advertised products or companies. According to these researchers, viewers react negatively when they sense they are being manipulated, but audiences usually do not notice the controlling influence of messages that are placed adjacent to content. Media programmers are thus able to manipulate what is "accessible in memory" by controlling message contexts.

Some researchers in psychology suggest that personality types should be included in media study so that researchers can better understand the influences involved between personality and media choice. For example, extroverts self-report that television does not substitute for other social contacts, while neurotic people see television as a way of passing time and having companionship. New technologies also may be used differently as extroverts may find computer interactions limiting of social contact, while neurotics may seek out social safety where they have control over the Internet. Perspectives of viewer personality may impact other psychology research that looks at the cultivation paradigm.

Cultivation researchers find, for example, that soap opera viewers (as compared to non-viewers) believe that society has higher rates of abortion, divorce, and extramarital affairs. Researchers also find that adolescent soap viewers are less likely to be concerned about pregnancies, STDs, and practicing safe sex. These researchers explain that since content analysis shows a high incidence of portrayals of unmarried sex on soap operas, there is reason to consider the cultivation hypothesis. Communications research perspectives of audiences, according to one researcher, can typically be grouped in one of three categories: structural (measures media influence on audiences), behavioural (analyses choices of decision-making audiences), and cultural (focuses on media used in cultural contexts).

Communications researchers using social judgment theory look at how the media are able to influence culture by getting people to buy into images to see themselves and others in particular ways. People "design or constrain [their] futures" based on their acceptance of meanings that are below the surface in media "archetypes, symbols, and images". Other communication scholars focus on message content evaluation, according to one researcher who states that while social psychologists are primarily concerned with social knowledge, and linguists with symbolic structures, communication scientists are concerned with the ways in which symbols affect social knowledge and vice versa. Despite disciplinary separations, some researchers find that various other disciplines have enriched communication science with multiple political, social, and cultural perspectives.

Rhetorical criticism, according to one scholar, provides methods to incorporate "identification and alienation" into communication theory. Another scholar suggests that communications research is enhanced by interdisciplinary perspectives including rhetoric and linguistics. Linguistic research perspectives see language as a signifying system that is constitutive of all knowledge so that thinking is constrained by language. For example, a language that uses only two words—black and white—for all colours, provides different possibilities of thinking and communicating than a language that has many words to describe colours. Linguistic research in semiotics looks at how visual signs, rather than language and the spoken word alone, influence the way people construct thoughts.

Semiotics looks at rapid-pace, multimedia images that viewers pick up on and make meaning of, oftentimes without thinking or questioning. Some linguistic researchers see semiology as a way of looking at how meaning is negotiated when message content interacts with viewer identity and socialisation factors. For these researchers, semiology finds ambiguity to be inherent in all communication because there is always the potential for multiple interpretations or polysemy. Linguistic researchers note that in the "extravagantly coded" messages of television, in which even a close-up shot can signify a meaning, research that focuses on shared meanings loses sight of potential ambiguity. These linguists point out that ambiguous programmes can be just as "manipulative" as an unambiguous programmes.

If a television programme, for example, is able to allow different audiences different interpretations of ambiguous messages, the ambiguity within the broadcast content makes the programme more influential because "it demonstrates its potency in a variety of cultural contexts". Comparative media theory also views the success of polysemy in mass media messages that do not have to be received in unison by an audience in order to be effective. Audiences are not empowered just because they have different interpretations of messages, according to one theorist who states that seeing the audience as interactive and choice-making ignores the way audiences are being kept from responding in a democratic way.

Many academics, regardless of their political ideologies, are concerned with responding to media influences that limit free speech and free thought. These academic researchers offer insights into the issue of media influence, not only on American teen sexual culture, but also on cultures around the globe. Academic research perspectives of media influence are grounded in the history of mass communications technology and the struggle to control its influence on society.

Communication Technology

Communication technology has had an enormous impact on society by changing the distribution of information and assimilation of knowledge. Communication technology has facilitated the evolution of "entertainment" that has reinforced or challenged societal norms since bards entertained audiences by reciting epic poems and oral histories. From the time of ancient Greece, linear print technology (alphabets) has altered oral practices and dramatically expanded the capabilities of language by preserving written records of thoughts and ideas.

Many centuries after writing was invented, the technology of the printing press enabled the first mass distribution of books, pamphlets, and newspapers that allowed single authors to inform and entertain large audiences. United States of America, facilitated by print technology, argued for democratic freedoms from government tyranny and fuelled the fight for American independence. In the newly established democracy, "freedom of the press" protections guaranteed that print media sources would continue providing information and influence. These protections were invoked, later in American history, when debates raged over the power and influence of new mass communications technologies. By the turn of the 20th century, electronic technology was at the centre of American political and social power struggles over entertainment's ability to propagandise masses of people in society.

From the time movie technology first appeared in 1894, censorship proponents sought to limit criminal and sexual content while other groups proposed using the new medium to teach social ideology. As early as the 1920's, movies were blamed for increasing youth sexuality. Movies were seen as reality-makers that clashed with values taught in school and contradicted societal norms. Studies during that time revealed that high school and college students were learning (and practicing) sexual techniques they had seen in the movies. Although censorship in the 1930s curbed sexual content in film, off-screen Hollywood sexual culture continued to influence American youth culture. The mass medium of movies was seen as a vehicle to propagandise audiences with entertainment messages.

In 1943, Elmer Davis, who was then America's Director of the Office of War Information, stated: "The easiest way to inject a propaganda idea into most people's minds is to let it go in through the medium of an entertainment picture when they do not realise that they are being propagandised". The mass audience reach of movies made them a battleground for numerous entities who wanted to promote a host of political and social agendas. Commercial interests soon became a major participant in the battle to wield mass media power in both entertainment and news.

Despite economic and political influences, radio broadcasters attempted to create a perception of neutral and non-biased news reporting, and Americans began to rely on commercial radio as their primary source of news and information. After commercial interests won control over radio in the 1920s, broadcasting began to create a national culture for shared consumerism. Although 1930s and '40s mass media images emphasised political rights and freedoms of speech, by the 1950s television stations did not want to air any content that would create controversy and affect advertising dollars.

In 1951, in order to avoid government censorship, the television industry's National Association of Broadcasters (NAB) adopted a code of self-censorship that created a proper moral image for television. However, advertisers soon became the greatest source of television censorship as advertising agencies for companies such as Procter & Gamble sought programming content that presented positive business images. By the 1960s, communications scholar Marshall McLuhan envisioned a shift away from the linear organisation of print media to the orality of television that he believed would revive oral communication as the basis for knowledge and knowing.

Television's high visual and audio impact, according to McLuhan, established new ways of meaning-making that reconnected viewers to the roots of oral communication. McLuhan anticipated electronic technology's potential to influence every facet of personal and public experience with fast-action, multi-sensory images that communicate more than many word. In the battle over media influence, movies and television have been, and continue to be, perceived as more powerful than print media. In the early days of film, movie theaters were not permitted to show news reels of certain volatile stories—such as violent labour disputes between union members and industry owners—that newspapers were free to cover. Although a Supreme Court ruling in the 1950s included movies under the free speech and free press protections of the First and Fourteenth Amendments, even today, cigarette and liquor advertisements are banned from television but not from newspapers and magazines.

The television medium became central in the power struggle to influence mass media content. Although commercial interests dominated television broadcasting, special-interest groups such as the National Association for the Advancement of Coloured People (NAACP) began challenging stations that did not give balanced treatment to certain issues. In 1966, the U.S. court of appeals ordered the Federal Communications Commission (FCC) to include more public input in licensing hearings, thus giving women and minority organisations the ability to advocate their agendas.

The struggle over media influence has included "government, private enterprise, advocacy groups, and, in more recent years, philanthropic foundations". In 1967, the Carnegie Commission proposed establishing the Corporation for Public Broadcasting. Foundations, and activists working in government and education, created the Public Broadcasting System (PBS) in an effort to shape a more intellectual culture. The issue of commercialised media continues to be at the forefront of debates over mass media influence on culture.

The evolution of communication technology has enabled fewer and fewer people to have greater and greater control over the distribution of information and entertainment. Both conservative and liberal scholars, educators, and activists are concerned with the mass media's ability to limit democratic discourse and propagandise through entertainment messages. Their perspectives inform potential solutions for mitigating the influence of mass media on American teen sexual culture.

A specter now haunts the world: a global commercial media system dominated by a small number of superpowerful, mostly U.S.A.-based transnational media corporations. It is a system that works to advance the cause of the global market and promote commercial values, while denigrating journalism and culture not conducive to the immediate bottom-line or long-term corporate interests. It is a disaster for anything but the most superficial notion of democracy. Through recent mergers, corporations have restructured media information sources into powerful global entities. Nine giant firms control the global media system including much of the Internet that was seen by some activists as a way to offset the globalisation of media monopoly. Merging media conglomerates are gaining increasing control over information as large corporations buy up small companies that fit with other corporate holdings.

Global media ownership takes power away from small, local news outlets and puts it in the hands of large corporations. Corporations that control mass media entertainment, news, and advertising are better able to manage information than many totalitarian governments. Corporate ownership has given mass media global reach that would be envied by anyone who wanted to limit free exchange of information in order to indoctrinate, propagandise, and control the thoughts of people in society. The successful propaganda of today's corporations goes unchallenged because media ownership "is based on a symbiotic relationship with a handful of media moguls like Disney, America on-Line/Time Warner, News Corp., and Viacom-CBS".

Corporations, with complete control over media news and information, have a considerable impact on free democracy. In an ideal democracy, all voices, not just those of the rich and powerful, should be heard. Media moguls' monopolisation of ideology, social culture, and the information that establishes these, interferes with democratic freedom of speech. American democracy depends on open debate and freedom of information that informs its "citizens who act to set the tone for the culture and the nation, through their votes, their opinions expressed in polls, their priorities expressed in how they spend money, and through their advocacy for or against issues".

Mass media interferes with this process by determining what gets discussed, what gets reported, and what is meaningful. In government and society, democracy requires two-way discourse so that audiences are not just receivers but responders. Americans tend to spend more time with mass media in their homes which further diminishes democracy by limiting discourse in public and private spaces. Media moguls control government through what one author calls "'corpocracy'-defacto government by mega corporations". In the United States, and in other countries around the world, people are often ignorant about media propaganda.

Entertainment and news broadcasts are continually influencing a public that believes it is not being influenced. People rarely consider what is put in by the media and what is "screened out". One scholar compares "corporate moguls peddling cosmetics, pharmaceuticals, and automobiles" to "Hitler, Mussolini, Hirohito, and Stalin," saying that "people today do not realise they are being programmed any more than did the people of Germany, Italy, Japan, and, later the Soviet Union". Current mass media ownership allows mega-corporations to manipulate information to promote political and social agendas that enhance corporate bottom-lines. Corporations are places of power where money and influence have instituted an unelected authority through which profiteers who control the global media grow richer and thus more powerful as they influence consumer buying.

Mass media have fostered a shared consumer identity through which we accept rather than debate what is happening in our world. Media-nurtured consumer culture encourages people to identify with media images, and to buy products to fit their media-based self-identities. This encourages individuals to identify with symbols such as brands of clothing, genres of music, and hairstyles that can unite diverse perspectives under a presumption of shared ideology. Corporations, such as General Motors, may capitalise on American symbolism—baseball, hotdogs, apple-pie, etc.—by advertising automobile ownership through standardised social conceptions. Symbolism not only stifles true social diversity, it helps stifle political diversity as well.

Political symbols can create perceptions of unity that divert attention from the lack of information on truly diverse perspectives. Too often, the sides with wealth, power, and influence are dead-locked in bipartisan political conflict that excludes multi-faceted viewpoints. The general public is encouraged to buy into political symbolism. Those who do not choose one side or the other are excluded in a voiceless void that pretends there are no alternate solutions—possibly because the issues are too complex for non-experts to understand.

Conflict without communication offers no hope of mediated solutions, only backroom deals that exclude the diverse voices of 'we the people' who theoretically participate in American democracy. When Americans buy products that are manufactured in countries that do not have American labour and environmental restrictions, corporations are able to maximise profits rather than ensure human safety and dignity or to protect the environment. By buying into a culture of consumerism that supports corporate profit, Americans widen the void between prosperous and poor both in the United States and around the world.

The impact of corporate-sponsored consumerism on global conditions of war, poverty, disease, and hunger is eclipsed by a corporate-run mass media that distracts attention from social and political issues and provides a corporate-biased view of information. Mass media-fuelled consumerism continues to encourage economic growth, according to one researcher, while it depletes resources and basically throws away everything except consumerism. Americans relinquish their ability -and responsibility—to think independently by accepting, rather than challenging, mass media information.

While the success of product placement in big-screen movies has given advertisers "enormous control" over movie content, it has offered even greater opportunities for corporations to cross-promote their own products. Now, corporate giants that own music, movie, and television media use entertainment to market their own music, videos, toys, and other products. The industry has built on this multipurpose-marketing so that entertainment becomes an endless line of tie-ins. According to one scholar, "the fashionable term for all of this vertical and lateral corporate integration is synergy, and synergy turns out to be just another word for monopoly". Synergy is a monopoly in which only the big companies are able to participate.

Mega-corporation synergy controls global media and information that impacts society. The blurring of the line between entertainment and advertising not only increases the marketing potential of entertainment but also decreases the information and usefulness of entertainment as advertising begins to "appropriate the icons and formulae of media content". In other words, marketing diminishes the potential of entertainment and news to provide information and messages that may be "democratically valuable". Corporate control has also commercialised news programming. What was once called "the separation of church and state" in the media referred to the separation of news from the influence of ownership in an attempt to allow journalists to cover the news and to make journalistic decisions. Corporate control influences what gets reported.

Corporations have control over the news, but present the appearance of separation between the corporate owners and the content of the information being distributed. News reports are now forced to be profitable so that journalist managers have been replaced with marketing professionals, and the boundaries between entertainment and news have virtually disappeared. News consultants, who have very secretive relationships with the news organisations that they serve, work behind the scenes to manage news content in order to attract viewers and build profits. The consultants' marketing data, gives them enormous influence over what was once journalistic decision-making.

International news is neglected because foreign bureaus are expensive and do not fit with the profit agendas of corporations. Although other mass media sources—print, radio, and cable television—provide varying levels of international news coverage, broadcast television networks are usually limited to the high-impact stories that concern a large number of Americans. Meanwhile, celebrity activity often obscures world news. For example, in 1977, entertainment news averaged 15% of total content on television evening news; by 1997, entertainment news averaged 43% of total content.

Mass media news increasingly focuses on celebrity gossip and viewer entertainment rather than information about the politics and technologies that are changing our world. Mass media virtually ignores stories about companies such as Monsanto that genetically alter crops and pump huge amounts of chemicals (drugs and pesticides) into food and water supplies. While incredible new advances in technology, science, and medicine offer prospects for a healthier future, they also present dangers of a Brave New World.

Corporate-controlled media focus Americans' attention on entertainment rather than news and information about these critical issues. In the new millennium, new media technology, including digitalised broadcast signals, cable television, and Internet access, have fragmented media audiences and further complicated media control issues. Mass media no longer entertains the masses. Unlike the early years of television, in which all Americans watched the same programmes, new technologies have enabled the fragmentation of media. Audiences have been compartmentalised into consumer packages through programming for specific interests.

Therefore, unlike earlier disputes over radio, movies, and television, when audiences had to share entertainment, audiences now can be isolated with their own preferred images of society. Scholars claim that even the Internet, which was touted as the new media information source for the masses, is succumbing to corporate control. People who hoped that the Internet would be a "cyberspace for the new millennium" may be disappointed as companies such as America On Line (AOL), with a 42% market share of America's home Internet service, exercise control by eliminating offensive chat rooms and shutting off user accounts. "Current trends toward Internet portals and the consolidation of media ownership," according to one scholar, "demonstrate that the tendency to control information and literacy is always at work".

The Internet has also become more and more about marketing as commercial forces are quickly turning search engines into shopping tools. While the public may be seeking information, what they're ending up with is more consumerism. Mass media's political and social influence on global culture impacts access to information, focuses on consumerism, and entertains audiences with sex and violence. Teens, and other mass media consumers, are encouraged to buy into the media images, to adopt media-generated identities, and to purchased the accouterments of those identities. Through entertainment, as well as other direct mass media advertising and marketing tools, teens are encouraged to focus on sex and purchase products that will make them attractive and popular.

Solutions for Media Influence

Although many scholars and activists agree that mass media influence threatens democratic discourse, their various solutions tend to be politically polarised. Some assert that a 1969 Supreme Court ruling guaranteeing First Amendment rights should prevent corporate monopolies from controlling mass media dissemination of information to the American public. They call for government regulation, noting that the United States is the only major nation to permit completely privatised ownership of mass media—even though the media have been given the responsibility for public information. They point out that the FCC, which is responsible for licensing and regulation, has increasingly permitted the corporate monopolisation of mass media, while legislative incumbents are pressured by media owners who can easily impact political campaigns. Some activists encourage citizens to lobby for media legislation that will seize power from commercial corporate giants and restructure the mass media.

Some advocate censorship, especially to protect children, while others argue that government censorship poses its own threat to free speech. Other solutions include:

1) FCC action promoting women and minority ownership of media;
2) low-powered, localised television and radio broadcasting;
3) community-access cable channels;
4) independent production and distribution of films;
5) internet "broadcasting" web sites; and
6) funding for Alternative Public Television (APT).

While scholars and activists debate political solutions to thwart mass media influence, many of them share an interest in educational solutions that teach media literacy. Media literacy, according to supporters, can incorporate competing political and social ideologies in order to foster critically aware citizens who are capable of political and social action. Media literacy can look at how media interacts with culture, society, and government to influence how audiences view the world, their society, and ultimately themselves. Both left-wing and right-wing ideologies see media literacy as a means for reestablishing democratic discourse among Americans who may be only marginally aware of mass media influence in their lives.

Media literacy may also provide an educational solution for the problem of mass media influence on American teen sexual culture. Media literacy in K-12 education can encourage students to question and challenge information sources and consider how mass media messages may impact individuals and influence society. It can teach aural and visual literacy that not only help students read complex, embedded electronic messages, but also help them create alternatives to mass media images. The United States lags behind other English-speaking nations that teach media literacy, according to advocates who encourage the development of educational responses to the proliferation of new communication technologies.

Technology in the classroom can provide educational enrichment for students who are accustomed to learning and communicating through technology. Media literacy can focus on making students critical consumers and creators of multimedia messages and allow them to interact with information in "multimedia, and hypermedia learning experiences". Media literacy in the United States is not a unified area of educational theory. Teachers' personal ideologies influence their approaches to media literacy and classroom education. Some educators believe that media education should challenge culture by teaching critical analysis as well as production, while others believe that students should be protected from media influences.

A surge of government funding in the 1970s directed research and teaching efforts toward critical viewing skills, and further direction came from funding for media arts and video production. In the 1980s, movement toward teaching core subjects severely diminished support for media literacy. However, there was a resurgence of interest as national government agencies for drug control, education, and health recognised media literacy's potential to teach students to identify and resist "inappropriate messages" relating to marketing, personal image, behaviours, and the depiction of society. By the mid 1990s, school standards began to reflect a new focus on communications skills and a growing interest in media literacy.

For example, the State of Minnesota added media literacy standards to the public school core curriculum, and the Pennsylvania State Board of Education approved goals that required students to be able to communicate and persuade, as well as discern propaganda and create their own persuasive messages. In 1996, the IRA/NCTE English Language Arts Standards recognised the need for students to work with oral, written, and visual communication. As state education departments, government agencies, and educators show increasing interest in media literacy, some advocates cite the practical problems of implementing K-12 media literacy education. These include time constraints of crowded curricula, inadequate teaching materials, and a lack of media literacy training in teacher preparation programmes. These advocates claim that educators in the classroom, rather than teacher education programmes, are building media literacy education.

Some media literacy educators reject academic resources that offer archetypes with strict standards. These grassroots advocates encourage teachers to develop their own teaching resources as an alternative to academic (or corporate media) curricula that reinforce social norms and the top-down distribution of hierarchical knowledge. According to these advocates, media literacy educators commonly "recognise that all media are constructed representations, that meaning is derived from the intersection of reader, text, and culture, and that messages have economic, political, social, and historical contexts". While some grassroots media literacy educators shun academic scholarship, others identify a need for academic research that informs practice and justifies media literacy education.

Some academic scholars, who share the concerns of grassroots educators, argue that media literacy "must be conceived as political, social, and cultural practice" that engages postmodern theories while recognising the hierarchy of educational practice. Educational reformers encourage a shift away from traditional top-down pedagogy toward a learning-centered approach for pre-service teachers to develop a deeper understanding, awareness, and critical attitude toward teaching practice that incorporates the knowledge and experience of students. This teaching practice, according to scholars, can transform the power structures in the classroom in order to access the knowledge of students who best understand the multimedia environment and their learning capabilities within it.

Postmodern perspectives may unite scholars with grassroots educators, but competing ideologies, politics, and research perspectives may pose an obstacle to the development of academic approaches to media literacy education. Although a broad range of academic disciplines contributes knowledge and research to media literacy theory, according to some media literacy advocates academics often "suffer from cultural myopia because of the limitations of academic specialisation and their own special-interest groups". These advocates criticise the lack of interdisciplinary cooperation that results in individual disciplinary perspectives that target "narrowly defined academic discourse communities".

English education, uniquely situated as the academic discipline responsible for language arts in the K-12 core curriculum, can provide a unified, multi-disciplinary programme of study that expands traditional literacy skills to include communication in non-print media. English teacher education programmes can centrally focus cross-disciplinary scholarly perspectives on the interconnectedness of mass communications, public discourse, power structures, and social cultures. As communication becomes increasingly computerised and electronic, some English scholars are revising the focus on printed text and written composition.

Some English educators suggest that using multimedia technology for teaching literary texts can give students a critical way of approaching sign systems and visual symbols. For example, hypermedia can be used to critically respond to literature using print, visuals, video, sound, and links to web sites. Other English educators advocate expanding the "deep reading" of print media to include the "deep viewing" of visual media. In some English programmes, students are developing critical skills to deconstruct mass media messages and practical skills to construct their own persuasive, multimedia communications. Although critical studies in English literature programmes can contribute to media literacy education, rhetoric—often located in modern composition and rhetoric programmes—provides proven analysis methods for both print and non-print literacy.

Rhetorical scholarship, historically situated in educational practices as well as democratic discourse, has evolved along with communication technologies since the early days of oratory in ancient Greece and Rome. Rhetoric, according to Aristotle, is "the faculty of observing in any given case the available means of persuasion". According to Cicero, the power of oratory persuades people and establishes civil order. Both Aristotle and Cicero focus on persuasion through orators' words as well as aural and visual aspects of performances.

Rhetoric's roots in a primarily oral culture provide analysis tools for decoding embedded messages and symbols in modern, multi-sensory entertainment that is designed to persuade a non-interactive audience. Rhetoric not only evaluates the content of mass media messages, it looks at the intent of mass media message-makers by focusing on both the purpose and method of persuasion. Teaching rhetorical analysis techniques can mitigate the influence of modern mass media on culture and democratic discourse by creating critical awareness. Thus, rhetoric can impact teen sexual culture by helping students discern specific influences of entertainment content and general influences of mass media.

6

Modern Media in Development

Internet and Agricultural Development

The Internet is not a panacea for rural and agricultural development, but it does bring new information resources and can open up new communication channels for rural communities and agricultural organisations. It offers a means for bridging the gaps between development professionals, rural people and agricultural producers through the initiation of interaction and dialogue. It can foster new alliances and interpersonal networks together with lateral and cross-sector links between organisations. Most importantly, it can support mechanisms that enable the bottom-up articulation and sharing of information on needs and local knowledge.

Primary benefits include increased efficiency in the use of development resources, less duplication of activities, reduced communication costs and global access to information and human resources. None of these benefits are guaranteed by the technology of the Internet. Instead, they are realised when people work together to make the most of a decentralised and accessible communication tool. There has been a rapid increase in the use of the Internet in developing countries.

With regard to rural and agricultural development and the Internet, organisations that support the betterment of rural populations and improvements in agriculture have important roles to play. For example, the Food and Agriculture Organisation of the United Nations, is playing an important role in assisting the establishment and growth of Internet services for rural communities and for agricultural development. In partnership with local stakeholders and other development agencies, organisations like FAO can help rural communities and agricultural organisations realise the benefits of improved communication and access to information. Enormous benefits await rural communities and agricultural organisations when communication improves between the non-governmental organisations, government services, private sector entities and educational institutes that support rural and agricultural development.

By sharing information about their activities in the fields of agriculture, rural development, forestry, fisheries, health, nutrition, and education, these agencies can better serve rural people and farmers. They can make use of "lessons learned," determine and use "best practices," and coordinate information about particular regions or successful development approaches. At the same time, rural communities and agricultural organisations can benefit equally from improved vertical channels of communication that enable rural stakeholders and farmers to communicate with decision-makers and others concerned with development.

An integrated approach to the expansion of Internet services will promote the necessary (but often neglected) horizontal communication between agencies linked to rural and agricultural development. At the same time, an integrated approach will provide the tools to enable rural people and farmers to enter directly into new vertical communication relationships with external agencies. Improving horizontal communication can improve the quality and relevance of information resources and physical resources available to rural people.

Improving vertical communication between rural people, farmers and decision-makers can improve the quality of decisions that affect rural communities and agricultural organisations. An integrated approach provides for vertical communication by establishing rural Internet access sites, and by enhancing horizontal communication between such entities as agricultural colleges, agricultural input and equipment suppliers, government extension services, rural development organisations, health care agencies, and agricultural research and documentation centres.

Improved horizontal communication can also include existing media services that serve rural stakeholders. For example, throughout the developing world, rural radio and, increasingly, television broadcast services, are important information delivery mechanisms. Their services improve significantly through the exchange of information and news by way of the Internet. African news items are commonly circulated among African news agencies via the Internet. Rural African radio stations are able to take advantage of Internet services to provide extension and rural development information from qualified research sources from around the world.

Internet services, in conjunction with existing and more widely used communication media such as rural radio, will enable the broadest enhancement of information and communication resources for rural people. For example, national or regional agricultural market information systems or extension information systems hosted on the Internet can be excellent information sources for the staff of rural radio stations throughout a region or nation. Using information on current market prices broadcast by rural radio stations, farmers can negotiate better prices from local buyers.

Improved horizontal communication and improved information resources can improve the quality of the decisions and interventions that impact upon rural people. At the same time, these improvements can enhance rural peoples' direct participation in development. Establishing rural Internet access sites and facilities in concert with efforts to enhance horizontal communication networks among the agencies involved in rural and agricultural development is the essence of the integrated approach highlighted.

Rural Connectivity

Electronic communication networks (ECNs) can be used to promote participatory exchange of information, knowledge and experiences at the grass roots level. ECN is a new medium of communication, and its casting and content need to be thought through. Participatory approaches can help in ECN design and use by all involved. Before looking at the details of why and how there could be benefits, it is important for us to understand what we mean by "participatory approaches".

There are many forms of participation, but the bottom line is that communities participate genuinely if they will derive benefits aimed at satisfying their real felt needs as they define them themselves. These benefits need not solely be material benefits—material benefits only make sense when they satisfy communities' fundamental needs such as subsistence, identity, freedom, protection, affection, understanding, participation, creation and leisure.

If participation is a basic need, it is worth looking at the typology of different types of participation so as to put the type of participation that empowers communities in the context of other non-genuine forms of participation. Structurally, villagers should have an understanding of the systems involved. They need to understand the system of networking they are involved in. This is important if they are to be empowered to get maximum benefit out of the system.

Some ECN materials may need to be tailored to specific audiences, but this does not preclude connection to the Internet although it focuses on immediate needs for purposes of encouraging participation and developmental objectives. A major issue is how the system will be designed to bridge the first mile with participatory approaches that use other media and channels to encourage people's inputting and receiving relevant information, knowledge and experiences to and from the network, even though they do not have direct access to the computer.

Through participatory rural communication appraisal, establish how 'a' wants communication coming from 'b', 'c', 'd', or 'e', to be packaged when it is received and the type of information wanted from each different point. The reverse is equally true; that is, each point can establish how 'a' can send particular types of information they need in terms of packaging. Electronic communication networking could easily supercharge the speed of everything from cash flow to customer services in a community. The network in this case is not only a means of facilitating business but the business itself.

Since important activities cannot be entrusted to one person, the community will need to be organised/ reorganised to deal with the new changes in communication. Changes in communication of this nature bring extreme changes like free-flowing information, and the community needs to be organised for this. Information is power, and investing it in few hands could disempower the other villagers. This can be overcome by group rather than individual training. Village activities are usually conducted under a big tree or in a big grass thatched enclosure with the people sitting together, circular fashion that is intimate.

Information received could be enlarged from a PC monitor to an overhead projector screen and the villagers could together or in groups discuss and strategise on what action to take next. As soon as they make their decision they could respond via the same medium. Juxtaposed to this is the possibility of the extension worker, the facilitator at village level, being an information worker too. This means people can still meet under the big tree or big grass thatched hut and discuss information they have received and plan together sending back replies.

However, the information worker will also play the role of decoding a lot of information, which could be difficult to comprehend or respond to. Although emphasis is placed on group activity, we should not make it seem a must. Whereas in nascent community organisations group approaches are strong, in emergent and mature community organisation decisions taken collectively are more and more delegated to individuals to implement or critique. If people cannot read and write it is not the end of the world. Programmes can be designed so that people understand interaction in the written word with regards to specific functions. This has been known to work very well with teaching bookkeeping to village groups involved in small-scale enterprises. Villagers are not concerned about into food security only.

A resource such as electronic communication network would be under-utilised if left for one function only. The people may like such a resource to be linked to development of other things like a library, information on opportunities for school leavers and entertainment. Participatory approaches could also establish different preferred information and communication needs. The systems, the technology itself and the atmosphere should be sensitive to the needs of women, men, children, adults and old people. If conflicts arise in use or content or type of technology, villagers would need to be familiar with conflict mediation and resolution.

Internet on Unconnected Rural Areas

The impacts of non-governmental organisations with Internet connectivity on rural communities represents an attempt to address the shortcomings of previous ICT evaluations. It is not meant to be a definitive study of how to examine rural communities' information sharing with NGOs possessing Internet connectivity, but it does propose a framework from which to build upon, improve, and make as relevant as possible an understanding of the benefits and impacts of the Internet for those who lack connectivity in rural areas of developing countries. Only through application in the field can such frameworks be tested, assessed, and improved upon.

It is hoped that this framework represents a fresh approach to understanding the complex issues and networks involved in information sharing and ICT use. Much of the literature on the use of information and communication technologies (ICT) concerns the potential that such investments offer for the developing world. Yet despite the rhetoric of how ICT can bridge the gap between the information haves and the have-nots, there is little research available that demonstrates that the use of ICT are in fact able to bridge that gap. Moreover, the focus of ICT research is currently fixated on the institutional level, which is composed of Internet service providers (ISPs), policy makers and governments.

While the value of such research is not challenged here, the fact remains that very little investigation has been conducted concerning the impacts of ICT on those who have the most to gain through the expansion of ICT in the developing world: the rural stakeholder communities. The benefits of expanding ICT to major urban cities has been well-documented, and the results of such urban investment can be seen in both the expansion of ISPs and the increasing connectivity throughout the cities of the developing world. Furthermore, the economics involved in development agencies' and corporations' willingness to expand Internet connectivity into rural areas in both Northern and Southern hemispheres has proven to be a major stumbling block.

In fact, rather than expansion being based upon the desire to meet the communication needs of rural communities, rural ICT expansion is primarily based on the degree to which it will be a profitable and worthwhile venture for the communication companies involved. The exclusion of rural communities and stakeholders from ICT expansion occurs in spite of the benefits that ICT is intended to bring to the isolated areas of the world. Even with the inclusion of the two questions relating to local stakeholders' acceptance, support, and ability to assume ownership of ICT, the CIDA report offers vague, insufficient analysis of the rural impacts of ICT.

This is evidenced in the presentation of a case study of a Peruvian rural telephone expansion project; the report states that the project's immediate impact is an increase in telecommunications access for 200 000 people. Beyond this statistic, however, the report was unable to identify any of the direct and indirect impacts of this project at the community level. There is a need to refocus ICT research so that the communication processes occurring with the use of the Internet are examined, rather than the infrastructural components themselves. Through learning how communities without Internet connectivity are able to benefit from organisations that have connectivity, and through learning how the two entities can work together to ensure that information is received, shared, and put to good use, those in development can move towards guaranteeing that stakeholders' needs are being met, and that adequate support is provided to those who need it most.

If the benefits of the Internet are not made available to the rural peoples who can benefit from it the most, "then we are failing to fully leverage the large infrastructure investments involved, and we are failing to assist people in making appropriate decisions based on such valuable information". The concept of participatory development communication is central to examining the use of the Internet as it relates to rural community stakeholders. Its basic tenet is that, "the communication process is more important than the production of media products".

Participatory communication for development is a process that emphasises a two-way communication process based on sharing ideas and information in order to improve the quality of life of the stakeholder communities. Unlike traditional communication methods of disseminating and transmitting information, development for communication "is about aiding different types of actors interested in understanding needs and assessing opportunities jointly; it is about providing them with the methods and media to reach common meaning, and about enabling them to negotiate with other actors with contrasting perceptions and interests".

The Internet is the latest in a long line of communication tools that enable a community to receive information and assistance from outside organisations. Unlike technologies such as radio, newspaper, and video, however, the Internet, "is the first media tool that allows every user to be a sender, receiver, narrowcaster and broadcaster". The tremendous opportunities that such technology can offer to rural stakeholder communities must not be missed. The challenge, however, is ensuring that the Internet is utilised for two-way communication processes such as communicating local knowledge and perceptions.

Current evidence suggests that to achieve sustainability and success, Internet projects for rural and agricultural development must begin with the real needs of the local community of users. This requires an approach that catalyses local participation, supports information and communication needs assessments, creates awareness of potential Internet uses, helps build communities of users, and facilitates locally managed, self-supporting communication and information networks. It also requires attention to capacity building and institutional strengthening for the intermediary agencies that serve rural populations so that they can make the most appropriate and creative use of Internet tools.

At the policy level, the success of Internet projects in development requires dialogue with national telecommunication agencies to help transform and liberalise the monopolistic telecommunication service environments common in developing countries. Monopolistic services tend to stifle the technological innovation, infrastructure investment and price improvements that often come with competition. Many analysts indicate that where telecommunication reforms have occurred, telecommunication services have "expanded and improved at a faster pace, productivity has increased, new services have become available, and in some cases, international capital markets have been tapped effectively.

A communication for development methodology typically begins with partnerships with local people and organisations to assist them in developing local communication processes by using tools such as community radio and small format video. At the same time, these initiatives work in concert with projects to create national agricultural information and communication networks that strengthen information sharing both horizontally and vertically. Such integrated approaches are achieving important economic and social benefits for rural users, while enabling national agencies to realise significant interorganisational efficiencies.

Communication for development methodologies deserve wider understanding. They are linked to participatory development methodologies and resemble basic computer systems analysis approaches which should start with the needs of computer users. Communication for development methodologies do, however, provide development planners with a conceptual approach that puts rural people, rural organisations farmers and agricultural organisations in positions where they can help direct communication and information network development.

An integrated rural Internet development approach also requires leadership among individuals who can put aside considerations of institutional competition. Such leaders must demonstrate, through action, their belief in the value of information sharing over information hoarding, and their dedication to rural and agricultural development. Without enthusiastic champions, most Internet projects will fail. It is not enough for development planners to build wonderful network systems and provide people with computers and modems.

Potential users must identify with a vision for beneficial applications, and they are most likely to respond to the visions of enthusiastic peers and colleagues. This vast project was initially led by only three young civil servants with a small budget and the support of a handful of high level government champions. In its early stages the project met with a great deal of resistance across many ministries.

Despite resistance, the project staff worked diligently to identify and empower institutional champions, most of whom were located at relatively low levels within the Government. Within two years, almost every Government ministry had at least one champion working to place useful information on the Internet and strengthen links between ministries and with the public. As the public became more adept at accessing available Government information, they began to demand more resources, while often providing vocal praise for the initiatives underway.

Before long, a momentum had developed that could no longer be resisted by reluctant bureaucrats, and eventually the provision of government information on the Internet became a matter of public policy. Parallel federal and provincial government efforts to strengthen community, private sector and educational access to the Internet helped push further demands for government information, along with mechanisms for engaging the government in new forms of electronic dialogue. Rural communities around the world tend to be under serviced in their access to the various technologies, Internet services and telecommunication connections that help transmit those services.

The Internet has sparked an unprecedented interest in telecommunication infrastructure among people who previously had little interest in telephone wires. A decade ago telephone systems could only be expected to carry voice conversations between two people. Now they are expected to move vast libraries of information, photographs, music and even video while enabling dozens of people to communicate with one another at the same time. Where once we could tolerate static and interference during a telephone call over poor rural telephone lines, we tend to become quickly frustrated by the very same lines when they are responsible for limiting our access to information and multiple communication channels. The demand for telecommunication improvement tends to be most acute among those who are most marginalised from information resources and communication services: rural people, rural organisations and farmers' groups.

People who once had very little interest in telecommunication infrastructure are now learning what they need to know to advocate for the communication and information tools they desire. In some cases, rural people and farmers take it upon themselves to create their "homegrown" services when established telecommunication bodies do not meet the demand. Evidence of this can be found throughout the developing world.

Communication Development Approach

FAO's twenty-five year experience with a communication for development approach to rural and agricultural communication, using media such as rural radio, small format video (participatory video), photography and print, is now being applied to the Internet in three small scale initiatives. This simple and common-sense strategy of involving people in assessments of their knowledge and communication needs is the cornerstone of communication for development methodologies. Much of FAO's success with communication for development approaches has involved the use of a medium that many development planners first dismissed as too "high-tech" and as being inappropriate technology. This medium is small format video (consumer grade video cameras and portable television monitors).

Facilitators use small format video to enable rural residents to articulate their ideas, aspirations, needs and solutions. Using video, people can speak directly to distant decision makers and researchers, gain access to knowledge presented in audiovisual form by experts (often other farmers), and share their experiences with one another across distances. In participatory video work, the communication process is more important than the production of a video. This aspect of the process is frequently misunderstood by observers of communication for development projects. It is not important for participants to become communication professionals: the goal is to provide media that are flexible enough to allow people to articulate and share their ideas.

Integrated into development planning activities, such a communication for development approach enables farmers and rural people to actively participate in development processes. These approaches enable rural stakeholders to articulate their knowledge, organise local activities, take part in decision making and fully recognise the value of sharing their ideas. Like participatory video processes, the Internet may help people to attain their development goals, but it must be used as a communication process tool and not simply as a static "information technology." Otherwise, Internet tools will be relegated to the junk heaps of inappropriate development technologies or dismissed because of previous failures to make the medium locally relevant and useful.

If, for example, the information outputs derived from highly technical electronic information systems such as famine early warning systems or food security databases are not made available to the people whose lives are the subject of those systems, then we are failing to fully exploit the large infrastructure investments involved, and we are failing to assist people in making appropriate decisions based on such valuable information. Before we even create such tools, we ought to involve the ultimate beneficiaries in determining the value of these initiatives and discussing planning approaches. A fact that is well known to current Internet users is that the Internet has the power to cut across social and geographic distance and help people find new ways of facilitating the flow of information and knowledge.

In many ways the Internet has always been a development communication tool. Within bureaucratic organisations it has a way of levering hierarchies, facilitating new communication patterns, and helping enable activities that might not otherwise occur. This factor makes it an especially attractive medium within communication for development efforts. The key to achieving similar results in new Internet and development projects is to begin with a grassroots, beneficiary-inclusive communication for development approach during the planning process.

The range of locally initiated Internet services in developing countries is remarkable. Many of these services have emerged with little or no external support, and many have become viable commercial services or not-for-profit services operated by NGOs. A large number of these Internet services have been around for almost a decade, coming into existence years before most donor agencies recognised any potential in the Internet as a development tool. Today, however, many international development agencies and international NGOs are finding ways to assist in the development and strengthening of local Internet services, infrastructure and information providers.

Despite the wide range of organisations supporting Internet services and applications in developing countries, obtaining accurate and up-to-date information on these activities is difficult. Donor agencies and project staff are not communicating about their initiatives very well. Despite the obvious potential of the Internet for sharing information on Internet projects, there is no single source that enables interested parties to quickly access information on specific projects, country activities and donor agency strategies and plans. As a result, the lessons being learned are being lost. Leaders in the donor agency community must remedy this problem soon to ensure that lessons learned are shared and that interested parties can quickly and easily identify opportunities for collaboration and for using Internet services and applications in developing countries.

The Internet was conceived in 1963 by Larry Roberts while he was working for the Advanced Research Projects Agency (ARPA) with funding from the United States Department of Defence. The fact that, at its essence, the Internet is a human relationship enhancement tool is reflected in its history, and the very human relationships of its early developers. ARPAnet, as it was called in the beginning, emerged as a communication tool in the late 1960s for a handful of Defence workers and contractors. It was designed as a fundamentally *decentralised* network in order to be a fail-safe communication system. Computers could send packets of information from one computer to another, across the United States, and those packets could travel through a variety of different routes to reach their destination.

If one or several routes were destroyed or malfunctioning, the packets would find alternative routes and eventually reach their destinations. The wife of one of the ARPAnet engineers was hearing impaired. To communicate with her while he was at the office and she was at home, the engineer used a telephone attachment that was then commonly used in the United States. A telephone text messaging device (TTY) enabled him and his wife to converse through text messages sent through the telephone system. This relationship enhancing tool influenced the engineer to incorporate text messaging between people (not just between computers) as a feature of ARPAnet. This feature became known as electronic mail or e-mail, and now millions of e-mail messages cries-cross the globe every day.

As a result of one person's positive experience with a similar relationship enhancing tool, what was initially a tool for computers to talk to computers became a tool for enhancing relationships. ARPAnet grew during the late 1960s and throughout the 1970s because new "nodes" and routes were added to reach university researchers. As a wider community of faculty members and students outside the Department of Defence began to use the tool, electronic mail quickly gained popularity across university and college campuses in North America. Because it was a decentralised network, there was little way to control its popular expansion, and it soon transcended its Department of Defence mentors.

The Internet today is a peoples' network. Anyone with basic computer equipment and a phone line can connect to it, communicate through it, host information on it, and look through it. Unlike many other media, such as television and radio, every user of the medium can be an information producer and knowledge sharer. No one knows for sure how many people are using the Internet today, but estimates range from 50 to 100 million people, and it is growing fast. In countries such as Thailand, Internet use is growing at a current rate of close to 1,000 percent per year.

The Internet is essentially millions of people connected together via millions of computers that are connected together. There are at least five million information-containing computers serving information to the millions and millions of Internet users. Each of those five million computers may contain thousands, or hundreds of thousands of pages of information. If current trends continue, there will be over 100 million computers connected to the Internet by the year 2000. Any one of those computers linked to the Internet might support one individual or thousands of individuals, together with the wealth of information they can contribute to the Internet. There are two powerful tools that form the basis of the Internet. The earliest on the scene, and still the most popular, is e-mail.

Using a simple address to guide them, e-mail messages jump from computer to computer, rapidly finding their way to their recipients. The more recent tool, and the one that has catapulted the Internet into popular culture, is the World Wide Web. The World Wide Web is the part of the Internet where we are witnessing the emergence of a vast global library of information. Electronic publishing of information on the World Wide Web is much less expensive than print publication. It is also very easy to become a provider of information on the World Wide Web and have people use your information almost instantaneously from virtually any location in the world. As a result, the World Wide Web is propagated with information on every subject imaginable.

In fact, an Internet user who wants to publish a work can do so for little or no money and make that work available around the globe. The World Wide Web is in its infancy, having only been developed in 1994, yet only three years after its birth it is one of the most popular information sharing tools in the world. Use of the World Wide Web is growing at a rate of 25 percent per month and it is estimated that some 100 to 400 new information sites are established on the World Wide Web each week. Prior to the World Wide Web, Internet users were limited to e-mail communication and cumbersome methods for retrieving files of information from other computers.

The World Wide Web changed that quite dramatically. Now we can retrieve information, documents, and a wide variety of audiovisual material simply by pointing and clicking. We do not even have to know the location of the computer from which we retrieve information. We just click on a highlighted word, or a picture, and within moments a document is transported to the screen in front of us. Some argue that the Internet's World Wide Web is humanity's second major communication revolution, the first being the Gutenburg Press in 1439. Compared to the costs of using telephones or faxes, communicating and sharing information using e-mail or the World Wide Web can be hundreds of times less expensive. Because information flows through the Internet in discrete packets of digital bits, those packets are able to share telecommunication lines with hundreds of other packets.

Where a traditional transatlantic telephone call will tie up a single phone line for only two people, an e-mail message can travel along a phone line with hundreds and even thousands of other messages. Some creative computer software developers have even made use of this feature of the Internet to create Internet telephone services that allow users to speak with other users around the globe, while completely avoiding long distance phone charges.

Twelve common elements can be identified among successful rural and agricultural Internet communication and information systems:

1. Preliminary participatory communication and information needs assessments with intended users.
2. Awareness building campaigns designed to sensitise decision makers to the possible uses of Internet services.
3. Executing agency commitment to participatory rural and agricultural development.
4. Local "champions" identified and supported.
5. Open participation of user community in design, implementation and management of communication and information services.
6. Institutional and user commitment to manage and sustain Internet services.
7. Involvement of the full community of users, including women and youth.
8. Ongoing provision for technical training, user support and outreach within the user community.
9. Combination of centralised and decentralised information production, analysis and distribution.

10. Ongoing provision for technical support and system maintenance/ upgrading.
11. User community financial commitment in communication and information systems (e.g. ownership of hardware, user fees, salaries, infrastructure, etc.).
12. Social service orientation of local private sector or not-for-profit (university or NGO) Internet service providers.

Local private sector or not-for-profit Internet service providers tend to be able to operate efficiently and profitably while providing customers with reasonable service prices. They are able to quickly troubleshoot and solve service problems, they can access capital through investment and credit (not as easily obtained with government-focused or donor agency services), and they are able to offer strong local user support, customer troubleshooting (often with house calls), and local training. Because they are dependent upon customer revenue for profitability, they are likely to respond quickly to customer needs and demands.

Government operated ISPs tend to be less able to meet customer needs and are often less responsive because they have other sources of support than customer fees. Local private sector and not-for-profit ISPs also contribute to the local economy and stimulate local interest in telecommunication through personal contacts and relationships. In 1994, as part of FAO's Latin American communication for development effort, community animators initiated an extensive participatory communication and information needs assessment among six hundred local farmers and their organisations.

The results indicated that farmers strongly desired an improved communication system, and local leaders required a better management communication system for organising activities and for agricultural and irrigation planning among 23 local organisations The farmers also wanted better methods for general communication and information sharing to assist in the planning of current and future work and activities. One strategy that they proposed was a computer-based communication system that would provide for both horizontal and vertical communication.

A communication for development expert from FAO provided initial logistical coordination and technical backstopping for the first nine months of the initiative. A computer network server was installed at the university and each farmer organisation was issued an account for dial-in access to a small pool of three modems connected to the server.

By June of 1996, 12 farmers' organisations were connected and using the system, several World Wide Web information services were available, and plans were being made to improve the system and involve all 23 farmers' organisations in the Rio Colorado Valley. Existing users make use of e-mail on a daily basis, and submit daily reports on irrigation quotas and planting activities to the local irrigation water authority. The farmers are proud of their community and its history, so they decided to organise a photography contest to collect historical photographs of the region and its agricultural heritage to place on their World Wide Web homepage.

They are planning to post their newsletters on the homepage as well, and hope to provide easy access to locally relevant market and weather information. Links will soon be made with the Technical Information and Communication Unit (TICU) to expand access to TICU's market information bulletin by placing bulletin information on the CETYS University server for access throughout Mexico and the world. These farmers' organisations have proven that Internet communication and information services are practical and beneficial when developed with full participation of users.

While the system has a long way to go in order to develop further applications and enhance user involvement with new applications, it is already attracting significant interest within the Mexican Ministry of Agriculture and other farmer organisations in Mexico. For example, Assistance and Services for Agricultural Marketing (ASERCA) is investigating the Mexicali experience in order to develop strategies for expanding farmer access to electronic information services related to marketing and the development of national and international trading links. There are even plans for developing an electronic trading system for agricultural products and services.

The development communication approach used to form the Mexicali system is the key to its initial success and its future sustainability. Using this approach has enabled the organisational leaders to fully understand the value of the system and its applications, and led to the farmers' decision to take ownership of the infrastructure and network development. These networks provide farmer organisations with data on crops, international crop status and market timing, prices, market conditions (regional, national, international), weather, technical and training information, and information about the various organisations that support their work.

The users also have full access to the Internet to find other information relevant to their lives and communities (e.g. health, social service, education, etc.), and they can use electronic mail to communicate with other farm organisations in Chile, as well as any of the millions of people using the global Internet. The most important aspect of this initiative is its specific attention to local information needs assessments, and provision of assistance to farm organisation personnel to help them develop the skills necessary to analyse and disseminate information that is locally relevant. This methodology emerged from previous development communication experiences using small format video, print media and rural radio.

It is very likely the most user oriented approach to developing Internet services in the developing world, and it is focused on rural and remote agricultural communities that would normally have little opportunity to access the benefits of Internet tools. Small information centres are located within the offices of farmer organisations and NGOs, and some of these offices are beginning to open up their Internet resources to non-agricultural community members such as youth groups and social service agencies. The network of users is currently small (five organisations and may become a model for the development of a much wider network within Chile, and, with some external assistance, throughout Latin America. Much of the information available through the Chilean network is useful to other Spanish speaking Internet users.

The Mexican and Chilean experiences are unique examples of using a communication for development approach to create horizontal and vertical communication systems for small producers and rural and remote communities. Throughout the other countries visited on the author's FAO fact-finding mission, it was generally observed that access to the Internet in rural and remote areas is emerging slowly. To their credit, many organisations in Africa, including FAO and its supported projects, are developing World Wide Web based information tools that may someday be of direct benefit to small producers and rural and remote communities.

In Zambia and Zimbabwe, for example, FAO projects are busy developing Internet-based market information tools, household food security information systems, famine early warning systems and ether sophisticated tools to assist decision makers. These systems are developed primarily by researchers and policy making bodies to fulfil their own internal information needs. Thus far, links to the ultimate beneficiaries of these initiatives are weak. In Africa, local and regional Internet service providers such as ZamNet (which also services the HealthNet project that connects rural health centres to the Internet), SangoNet, MangoNet, Enda-Dakar and Internet Africa, appear to be the only organisations with the tangible experience of providing Internet services to organisations and individuals in rural and remote areas. Their track records speak for themselves. They have managed to provide Internet services to many of the intermediary organisations that serve small producers, rural communities and agricultural organisations.

Many of the field officers of UN agencies and multilateral donor projects make use of electronic mail and Internet information services provided by these local services. The individuals who work within these Internet service providers tend to be extremely dedicated to their work and to improving Internet service in Africa. These services are "natural" examples of the horizontal and vertical communication channels essential to the integrated approach. Future Internet development activities for rural communities and farm organisations in Africa and Latin America ought to begin with the experiences and services of existing Internet service providers and existing user groups. There is a wealth of experience, talent, creativity and local understanding available, and development agencies would be wise to utilise these resources at every opportunity.

SMALL AND MEDIUM ENTERPRISE DEVELOPMENT

Private sector businesses, large and small, are using the Internet to reach new markets, promote products and services globally, and access critical business and financial information. Rural food producers in North America now use the Internet to sell a wide variety of products including live lobsters and packages of apples, oranges, grapefruit, cheeses, smoked meats, pastries and pies. Producers of rural crafts and manufactured goods sell everything from clothing to furniture over the Internet, and use the Internet to organise support networks.

The Internet represents a global storefront for such rural and remote businesses, providing them with a degree of access to customers never before possible. The tourism sector has been quick to recognise the benefits of the Internet for advertising destinations, tours and holiday services. For all of the countries visited during his recent FAO Internet fact-finding mission, the author was able to make use of World Wide Web travel information from the host countries in order to make travel plans. With full colour pictures, and information on hotels, weather, attractions, events, travel tips, currency conversion rates, visa information and much more, travellers are able to obtain timely and accurate information and make informed destination choices.

Of particular interest are the World Wide Web sites for "ecotourism," game parks, and adventure tours in rural areas of Southern Africa where rural tourism is a growing industry. Tourism operators in rural and remote areas have a difficult time marketing their destinations through traditional media due to production and distribution costs. The Internet now represents a very inexpensive way for them to showcase their sites to the world and interact directly with potential tourists.

The news media in developing countries have also been on the forefront of developing Internet applications. Internet service providers (IPS) use the Internet to source news stories from local writers in developing countries and share those stories with international wire services such as Associated Press. IPS is also able to provide Internet feeds that enable African news media to have access to African news from around the continent. This is particularly relevant to rural radio stations and other rural newspaper and newsletter producers that would otherwise have been unable to obtain the same news from other sources. IPS can also provide an outlet for rural news writers to share their stories regionally, nationally and globally. Similar Internet strategies for rural radio networks, which might also incorporate digital audio transmissions, may well emerge in the near future.

At the end of the Twentieth Century, people in rural and remote areas of developing countries are facing many unprecedented challenges brought on by the changing global economy, dynamic political contexts, environmental degradation and demographic pressures. The number of food insecure around the world continues to increase. To deal with these challenges, and to make critical decisions, people at all levels of society, and especially the food insecure and the organisations that serve and represent them, must be able to access critical information and communicate.

Improved communication and information access are directly related to social and economic development. Participatory development is fully dependent upon communication and information sharing processes. One cannot expect poor farmers and food insecure residents of rural communities to list computers and digital telecommunication services as high priority items for improving their lives. However, there exist various intermediaries that serve these populations which, together with small and medium enterprises (SMEs) in rural areas, can take advantage of these technologies to improve their work, improve communication capacity, gain efficiencies and reduce telecommunication costs.

An integrated approach that fosters horizontal and vertical channels of communication is key to insuring that such benefits are realised. Intermediary organisations such as extension field offices, rural NGOs, health clinics, government offices, and church organisations together with SMEs, can offer benefit to their rural client groups in numerous ways. Strategies for improving Internet access and use for rural and agricultural development will necessarily involve full participation of intermediary organisations and other rural stakeholders. As Internet services become more widely used among these organisations it becomes more important to facilitate the exchange of lessons learned and best practices that emerge from on-the-ground experience.

The following are the 11 activities to assist rural stakeholders in gaining access to, and developing creative uses for, Internet services:

- Promote regional coordination of Internet strategy for rural and agricultural development.
- Establish pilot projects.
- Use a communication for development approach.
- Support efforts to liberalise telecommunication policies in developing countries.
- Support local Internet entrepreneurs and other service providers in developing countries.
- Assist stakeholders in advocating for Internet service provision and telecommunication infrastructure and policy improvements.

- Orient existing Internet information services to users in developing countries.
- Support rural and agricultural education sector Internet capability.
- Provide Internet awareness building and demonstration.
- Support rural and remote infrastructure development.
- Support creative Internet applications and information services for rural and agricultural development.

Video and Audio Technologies

Video and audio technologies have become smaller, cheaper, more reliable and easier to use, making them accessible to many organisations and to individuals, and usable in many different contexts by a wide range of people. Running parallel to this has been a change in development thinking towards sustainability of livelihoods and the participation of rural and urban communities in decision making about their own lives. Moves towards participatory development and the desire to make development a reality for the disadvantaged, especially women and the "poorest of the poor," have necessarily meant changes in approaches to media: to its role, the technology used, the skills needed, who it is for, and the role of the community and the media professionals.

The polarisation of media into professional and people-based media with opposing characteristics is now breaking down and being replaced by a continuum of participatory approaches involving different groups of people with a range of skills able to respond to changing needs and contexts. The "professional media" end of the continuum is still with us, but more and more examples are now available which show that there is a wide range of use and users. Media communication is no longer seen as simply a top-down flow of information, exemplified by the delivery of messages through the national press, radio and television to health and agricultural extension services or to mobilise populations behind government development programmes.

Nor are populations regarded as one mass to be blanketed with the same message, but rather as communities with differing needs and perspectives on the world It is no longer considered good enough for media professionals to isolate themselves from the audiences they are supposed to serve. Now they can be found working with local populations to determine their needs in relation to the broadcast media; they are involved with trainers and trainees in the development of training materials, and are facilitating community use of media to explore situations and make development decisions. Their working practices share many of the "salient techniques and characteristics should be considered as elements in a paradigm designed to be useful to community radio projects".

Changes in working practice have been facilitated by the development of participatory methods such as "rapid rural appraisal" which enable outsiders and communities rapidly to share experience and learn together. Where once the questionnaire survey and statistical analysis were the main means of investigation and analysis, there is now a mix of methods which are not dependent on literacy and high levels of numeracy. For organisations seeking to practice participatory development, in which the development of communicative capacity and horizontal and upward flows of information are emphasised, new technologies that rely less on technical skills and more on sophisticated but easy-to-use equipment can be dynamic tools. Such technologies have enabled non-professionals to become skilled at using media, opening up great opportunities for them to have access to, and control over, the tools for information and communication generation and exchange.

However, although participatory approaches to media have been around since the 1960s and new approaches are constantly being pioneered, their sustained use in development programmes and projects is still some way off. A task for the 1990s should be to "come up with a set of core ideas and principles of participation and communication...." Such a core set is really dependent on the exchange and analysis of a wide range of practice and experience. Although he was writing of radio, we could apply this to media work across the board.

Communication Development

Communication and development theory, provided us with a model for an audience participation approach to designing messages for development communication backed up by a wealth of personal experience, to produce a handbook on rural radio. This has led to the establishment of a Creative Radio for Development network on the Internet. Although there is now a wealth of experience around, and people are starting to share it, we still are lacking a good, universal mechanism for dissemination. The processes of production for a training course based on video by the Agricultural Information Centre (AIC), Kenya, shows what might be called a conventional training institution media unit operating in a participatory way.

Their working practice enables them to provide training materials based on short "trigger videos", which help people to examine actions directly related to their working life and, through discussion, decide on ways to improve things. Interest in the use of radio is very high at the present time, and considerable effort is being placed on training in new ways of working. However there are many obstacles which can mean good training goes to waste as the new skills cannot be put into practice. Participatory work necessitates a close interaction with communities and money has to be found to visit and if necessary stay in rural areas.

Lack of infrastructure can mean that only those living near roads and cities are reached for consultation and evaluation work. Radio and video have been part of development communication for many years and their use has changed in response to the new approaches to development and to changes in technology. It may seem obvious, but short-term projects that take no account of the local ability to pay once the project is over lead to dead technologies around the world. Training remains a critical issue. In relation to equipment there is a need for maintenance and trouble-shooting skills. In relation to use there is a need for people to be able to create as well as use information and education materials, which calls for other skills, and possibly new kinds of training. An approach to training which focuses on job related skills can result in new skills being released into the commercial marketplace rather than being used to benefit the organisation or community in which they were trained.

Education in Rural Areas

Public services, such as education, health care and social security, are virtually nonexistent in rural areas in many developing countries, and many countries are cutting back on government spending for such services. In the industrialised world, new technologies and resources for distance education and technology-supported learning, as well as for distance health care (remote consultative networks), are being developed at an increasingly rapid rate. The vision is to develop global or regional resource banks that allow everyone, anywhere, to consult specialists, find the information and learn what he or she needs, when it is needed. Telecommunications is an indispensable tool for all the above services and activities.

"Plain Old Telephone Service" (POTS) would help, as indicated above, but access to advanced services, such as fax, electronic mail, electronic document interchange (EDI) and access to bulletin boards, computer-mediated conferences, databases and ultimately two-way video and multimedia resources would make a tremendous difference. Radio and television broadcasting, including community-owned and controlled local radio stations, also offer the possibility to bring education and training programmes to isolated areas. Broadcasting also offers a means to promote cultural development and entertainment for people in isolated rural areas.

Therefore, the planning of broadcasting infrastructure should also be part of integrated rural development. Effective international cooperation for sustainable development, ranging from community development and combating the spread of epidemics and drug abuse to disaster relief and global environment watch programmes, depends on the availability of adequate telecommunication infrastructure in the developing countries. Regional cooperation and large scale programmes for sustainable development concerning, for example, new methods of production of energy from waste, development of biochemical fertilisers or the promotion of new patterns of consumption, need tools such as e-mail and computer-meditated conferences to share experiences, to involve community politicians and other "major groups" in the decision-making process, and as fora for continuous dialogues on issues of common interest.

Also, the thousands of ongoing and new initiatives by non-govern-mental organisations and individuals involved in community development would benefit tremendously from the possibilities offered by such tools to better coordinate their efforts and to create more synergy. Availability of advanced telematics services in rural areas would enable governments to maintain up-to-date information about climate, health hazards, and other issues related to environment and sustainable development in databases that could be accessed by concerned authorities, organisations and global "watch programmes".

Development agencies can only be physically present for a limited time at the site of community development projects. It is becoming increasingly clear that easy access to expertise and "knowledge networks" is essential for development to be sustainable after projects come to their inevitable end. Consequently, the paradigm for international cooperation is gradually changing from dependence on the traditional time- and space-limited "technical assistance" projects to rely more on sustainable collaborative networks. To introduce computers and advanced telecommunication services in rural communities, where people live the way their ancestors have for generations and are lacking even basic education, may appear inappropriate and too sophisticated.

However, if rural areas should be able to compete in attractiveness for business, social and cultural activities with the large cities, rural communities must be provided with at least the same services at the same costs as those provided to the urban population. Arguably, rural communities need even better services to compensate for their geographical isolation and other "penalties" of being far from the cities and markets. There is always a risk that this will further increase the gap between the "haves" and the "have-nots".

Many economists argue that increased competitiveness and profitability of local enterprises will create new and better paid jobs and ultimately benefit the whole nation and improve the living standard of the population as a whole. This, however, will depend on the existence of adequate policies, regulations and legal frameworks that ensure a fair redistribution of wealth and "universal access" to telecommunications. "Universal access" to information and networks would give ordinary people more power because through such networks they can participate in informal, user-driven action groups and decision-making structures, which cannot be controlled by anyone. In the long term, this may radically change the role of politicians and enhance democracy.

The main obstacle to providing telecommunications at a large scale in rural and remote areas is not lack of technology nor even lack of money. If there is a profitable market in sight, the huge investment required to build the networks will probably come forward, even though some economists claim that capital is running short globally. True, the cost of providing telecommunications in rural areas is higher than in urban areas, but new technologies promise to make rural telecommunications more cost-effective in the near future. However, a market that can bear the cost does not yet exist, and many countries need to change their policies to create a more attractive investment climate.

Access to the "information super highways" is therefore presently an obstacle which must and could be overcome by new technologies, providing there is a market for advanced telematics services. People in rural areas in poor countries and are quite unaware of the advanced telecommunication services available today and of the benefits of using these services, as are many people in rural areas in industrialised countries. Other formidable obstacles are the lack of skills to use such services and the absence of user support. Therefore, the business of providing basic, let alone advanced telecommunication services, to a few isolated customers in rural areas is likely to be relatively unattractive for still some time.

Presently, it seems that the only realistic way of providing advanced telecommunications and telematics services and the required user support in isolated rural areas is by concentrating such services to a focal point in the community. Even if the service of such a focal point will be limited initially to POTS and telefax, there will be a real need for more advanced services, as indicated above. It is also important to have a vision for meeting those needs that appeals to government decision-makers across the various occupational sectors as well as to telecommunication equipment and service providers. Just imagine what such a telecentre could do for sustainable development of rural areas and for bringing people in remote areas in touch with the rest of the world.

It could be used for data processing, for accessing databases by small local enterprises and individual entrepreneurs. If properly equipped, it could also be used for "tele-training" and for "tele-health care" so that the local inhabitants could learn new skills and get medical advice when needed. Telecentres are also likely to become centres for cultural and social activities, particularly if they are equipped to receive TV and sound broadcasting. Availability of advanced telematics services in rural areas would not only contribute to reducing the urbanisation process, but may even reverse the trend by making it possible for enterprises to locate some of their business in otherwise isolated areas.

The community telecentre could very well function as a remote office for "tele-working," shared by several city-based companies. This would contribute to attracting skilled people (back) to the rural areas and to reducing transport of people. Such educated and trained individuals are needed to sustain the process of development and change, once the international and government support required to initiate community development is withdrawn. The community telecentre could, in geographically widespread and sparsely populated areas, be used as a local hub to which public (and private) telephones located at strategic points covering the area are connected. It could also be complemented with paging systems so that villagers can be notified of incoming calls. The concept has already been successfully tried out in rural and isolated areas in many developed countries, e.g., in Scandinavia, the UK, including northern Scotland, Ireland, Australia, Canada, Japan and USA.

The "telecottage" movement is steadily gaining momentum and national associations of such community telecentres are being formed. Such associations constitute a network for mutual support, through which new telecentres, established in the developing world, could connect with people with similar problems and experience of various aspects of community development. There are needs for telecommunications in rural and remote areas but there is not yet a "market". Clearly, access to advanced telecommunications has little meaning unless people have a use for such tools. This means that the introduction of telecommunications in rural areas must be done as part of a concerted effort by all concerned government sectors to develop a rural community or region.

Telecommunication development in rural areas will only have a significant impact if it is part of a larger effort of community or rural regional development. Conversely, community development projects are much more likely to be successful if supported by adequate telecommunications. Development of a community is primarily the responsibility of its inhabitants and of the government concerned. However, a minimum of resources and some external "change agent" is usually required to develop the necessary capacity for community development to "take off". The international community, including the private sector, has good reasons to assist in this process.

Thus, community telecentres must be introduced as part of a concerted effort of community development, in close cooperation and partnership with the community inhabitants, the concerned governments, concerned international and non-governmental organisations, as well as with private sector stakeholders. If community telecentres are to be used as distance learning centres for local people to learn skills relevant to rural community activities, cooperation and contributions must also be sought from the numerous organisations and institutions involved in the development of relevant "open flexible distance learning" resources.

The ability to view immediately one's own self speaking on videotape assists individuals to see themselves as others see them. This self-image conveys the impression immediately that one's own knowledge is important and that it can be effectively communicated. These video techniques create a new way of learning, which not only build confidence, but show people that they can say and do things that they thought were not possible before. For those who cannot read or write, these video techniques make available information that people can understand. They also create new communication links. People can talk with other people in different villages, with other people in different social or economic classes, with other kinds of experts, or with bosses.

Video in the hands of a skilled community worker can assist people to talk to other people with whom they may have never before had any communication or access. It can remove the inherent threat in communicating with persons of authority. It can assist in the planning of action and in the resolution of conflict, potential or actual. The very presence of a community worker with this technology shows or provides a sense of caring and involvement which enhances the willingness of village people to become involved in new ways of learning and doing.

The community worker and the video process bring people together for common cause, create new information channels and inspire a belief and confidence in self-help. There are times, however when video as a tool is inappropriate to a particular situation. For example, the field-worker may be called upon to arbitrate between difficult interpersonal relations within an organisational framework or project, in which using video could actually interfere with sensitive needs which require immediate action. A community worker must be attuned to such situations and know when to make the decision to use or not to use video as a communication tool.

Video production and utilisation equipment that is most appropriate for development workers and educators is not the same as that used for broadcast purposes. It is less expensive and the technical quality of the image produced may not be as high as broadcast equipment; however, community use of video does not require as high technical standards. It is the message, more than its packaging, that is important in community work. It is important to recognise that there is a wide range of non-broadcast video equipment on the market. This is a highly competitive field, with the technology changing very rapidly and manufacturers constantly developing new models, so great care must be taken to select the most suitable equipment for the purposes for which it is to be used. It is also important to make decisions that are as "long term" as possible. Unfortunately, the video industry looks on three years as "long term".

Different Learning Types

This is a form of learning in which country residents use their experience and knowledge to teach one another, or member of one community use their experience and knowledge to teach other communities. An example of the use of video in this form of learning would involve the production and screening of a videotape made by farmers in one village to assist farmers in another village solve a problem concerning marketing. This form of learning is informal and in direct response to a community's perceived needs.

Vertical learning: Vertical learning is usually associated with formal learning involving a teacher and students. In community work video is often used for this form of learning to give technical training, or provide information from external expertise. The videotapes are made with specialists in a variety of fields. An example of the use of video in this type of community learning would be the screening of a series of videotapes in the community on the subject of nutrition made by an expert in nutrition from a university or the ministry of health.

Exchange learning: Exchange learning involves the interchange of information, ideas, techniques and knowledge through interactive as opposed to one-way communication. In this form of learning teachers become learner/teachers and those who are traditionally regarded as learners become teachers as well. This process enables the exchange of views, opinions, information and knowledge with a specific objective in mind, such as improving understanding, creating group consensus, and pointing ways to effective actions. Videotape recording equipment is very portable, making it easy to transport and to use in villages and barrios.

It is closest to movies in terms of media advantages in community work. It is light, easier to learn to handle, becoming less costly and has one very important advantage over film: it does not need to be sent away for processing in a film laboratory but can be played back immediately, in much the same way as audio-tapes, on a tape recorder. With video, however, there is a moving image as well as sound. In the hands of a skilful community worker, portable videotape recording equipment is a tool which can greatly accelerate the process of self-help and learning.

As a catalyst for community action, video can assist in changing the human condition as well as describing it. Community workers can use video in a number of ways. One way is to use it within a village to show individuals or groups what they already know. Used this way, video becomes a mirror. It is through such videotapes the community worker can help individuals or groups analyse what they are saying about their own hopes and problems. Video assists village people to look objectively and more clearly at their own statements. Another thing community workers can do is to take videotapes they have made with one village group and show them to the same kind of group in another village.

Video made with the assistance of the community worker and shown from village to village amongst people of the same background becomes a new form of learning. This is known as horizontal learning and is becoming increasingly acknowledged worldwide as an essential component of education, usually (but not exclusively) among adults. Village people can use video to teach themselves, from within their own village, or between their village and other villages, and they are doing this increasingly.

Vertical communication: Sometimes the community worker and the people use video to speak to people of authority, to people who are regarded as having power over common village people. In like manner, the community worker uses videotape with such people to talk back to the common people of the village. In this way, new communication links are sometimes established and groups and individuals who normally have not been able to talk to each other are able to do so and to learn from each other.

7

Internet and the Society

The Internet is an important part of the infrastructure for the global information society. The Internet is an economic and political factor whose further development and regulation will influence the live of everyone decisively. Hardly visible in the stir caused by the conflict among the Internet giants Microsoft, Netscape, Oracle, IBM, CISCO and others, the Internet Society has undertaken the task to shape and advance the technical, political and cultural future of the Internet. The Internet Society regards itself as the international organisation which furthers the global cooperation and coordination for the Internet, its technologies and applications. Everyone interested in the further development of the Internet can become a member of the Internet Society. Conferences and technical and political bodies give ample opportunity to exert influence on international and national level. Individual members who want to participate in shaping the medium's future are equally welcome as companies which use or offer the Internet as modern technology for their purposes.

The standards for communication in the Internet are defined in the Internet Engineering Task Force (IETF). More than 80 working groups in 8 fields of work are concerned with specific technical subjects. IETF does its work during three big meetings of more than 1500 participants per year and by means of all the communication means provided by the Internet. On behalf of ISOC and the Federal Network Council (FNC) of the USA, the central resources of the Internet, eg names, addresses and protocol parameters have been managed by the Internet Assigned Numbers Authority (IANA) under the direction of Ian Postel, who tragigcally died last summer. Currently ISOC is intensively involved in restructuring the management of these resources within the new organisation ICANN (Internet Corporation for Assigned Names and Numbers).

Government policies are being debated and enacted, marketing and programming strategies are being developed, and services for children are being designed. If we are to believe some hyperbolic visions of cyberspace, the information superhighway will be a great equalising force that will bring unprecedented opportunity for all. Improvements in education and other benefits for children are often at the center of these visions. But history offers us cautionary lessons. In this century enthusiasts have hailed every new medium-from radio to FM to television to cable to satellites-with claims that it would reinvigorate our culture, expand educational opportunities, and enhance the democratic process. None has lived up to these claims. In each case, powerful commercial forces have used civic values to gain support for the new medium-and then squelched the very policies necessary to serve the public good. While traditional media are sometimes viewed as unnecessary diversions, digital media will soon become an integral part of daily life. Those without access to the communications system are likely to fall behind in education and be unable to compete in a highly selective job market.

Yet just as access is becoming imperative, the number of children living in poverty, with little or no access to technology, is growing at an alarming rate. Access isn't the only challenge; the quality of the new media culture for children also raises concern. Unlike TV, online media are dynamic and two-way. This participatory quality makes them particularly compelling to children. Such technological breakthroughs as real-time audio, real-time video, and virtual reality modeling language are transforming online media. Eventually, this interactive online world could supplant traditional television as the most powerful and influential medium in children's lives. Many online services are now available that seek to challenge children by exposing them to places, people, and ideas far outside their everyday experiences.

For example, Plugged In, a Web site created by a community computing center in Palo Alto, California, allows poor children to explore the Internet, produce their own art, and display it to other children around the world. Another Web site, CyberKids, enables children to write and share their own stories in an online magasine. Special networks have been established to foster online communities for children. These educational and civic services, however, are in danger of being overshadowed by a powerful interactive commercial culture with an unprecedented ability to capture children's attention. Marketing to children has become a multibillion-dollar business.

The direct spending power of children, almost all of it discretionary, has risen rapidly in recent years. In 1995, according to Interactive Marketing News and Youth Markets Alert, children under 12 spent $14 billion, teenagers another $67 billion, and together they influenced $160 billion of their parents' annual spending. In the last decade, these trends triggered a proliferation of new TV networks aimed at capturing a segment of the hot children's market, including the controversial classroom news service Channel One, the highly profitable Nickelodeon cable channel, CNN's Cartoon Channel, and the Fox Children's Network.

Character licensing has become the driving force not only in children's television, but also in much of the rest of children's culture. Cross-promotion of licensed products through TV, movies, magazines, discount stores, and fast food restaurants has produced a proliferation of licensed characters that permeate every facet of a child's life. The new online services for children are being developed in the context of this highly commercialised children's media culture. Children are a disproportionately important market for the new interactive media because they are early adopters of high-tech products. As an executive from Saatchi and Saatchi, a leader in the online kids' marketing field, recently proclaimed, "There is nothing else that exists like it for advertisers to build relationships with kids." Advertisers are already aggressively moving into cyberspace.

In US a Coalition for Advertising Supported Information and Entertainment (CASIE), led jointly by the American Association of Advertising Agencies and the Association of National Advertisers, is spearheading lobbying efforts to ensure that advertising becomes the dominant mode for funding online content and to ward off government restrictions. The coalition claims that advertiser support for online services is the only way to make information services affordable to all. But the consequences of making advertising the key to universal access for children are troubling. Advertisers are not just supporting online content; they are shaping much of the virtual landscape for children. At Saatchi and Saatchi, psychologists and cultural anthropologists have perfected a variety of techniques-including play groups, art, and games-to probe children's feelings and behavior when they go online. They are also studying the nature of "kids' culture" as a separate set of experiences and values from that of adults.

Knowing that children often use computers alone, marketers are carefully cultivating this separateness in the design of online services that circumvent parental authority. One online children's service recently published results from a survey that asked children whom they trusted more-their parents or their computers. The majority of respondents said they put more trust in their computers. According to advertising researchers, going online quickly puts children into a "flow state," that "highly pleasurable experience of total absorption in a challenging activity." This is an optimal condition for advertisers to reach children.

Traditional commercials will not work online. "Anything that is perceived as an interruption of the flow state," explained a Saatchi and Saatchi executive, "whether it's artwork being downloaded or an ad that is obtrusively splattered on a screen, is going to get a negative reaction." So the solution is the seamless integration of content and advertising in "branded environments." The goal of these environments is to "get kids involved with brands"- including "brand characters, brand logos, brand jingles, and brand video." Major children's advertisers have Web sites where children are encouraged to come and play for extended periods of time with such product "spokescharacters" as Ronald McDonald, Kellogg's Snap, Crackle, and Pop, and Chester Cheetah. The aim is to encourage children to develop ongoing relationships with the characters-and the products.

The new interactive media are being designed to compile personal profiles on each child to help in developing individually tailored advertising known as "microtargeting" or "one-to-one marketing." The sites get children to volunteer such personal data as e-mail address, street address, the identity of other family members, and purchasing behavior and preferences. Sophisticated computer software can track every move a child makes online and give marketers "clickstream data" or, in the vernacular of the business, "mouse droppings."

Marketers can pursue children with few restraints. Nothing prevents them from collecting personal information from children and selling it to third parties. The lines among advertising, entertainment, and information-already dangerously blurred in television and other media-are likely to disappear entirely in the new online environment. "What is really happening," explains one industry expert, "is what will ultimately happen on interactive television: the infomercialisation of all programming." Even traditionally noncommercial services are likely to be shaped by the norms of this new unregulated media environment. While laws prohibited from most forms of advertising on television, there are no restrictions on its use of advertising online.

Hate Speech and Free Speech

The Internet has been rightly hailed as a groundbreaking interactive marketplace of ideas, in which anyone with the necessary hardware and software can set up a cyber-stall. But the downside of this unparalleled information exchange is that, alongside its many valuable online resources, the Net also offers a host of offensive materials - including hate materials - that attempt to inflame public opinion against certain groups of people. This section explores the ways in which hate-mongers use the Internet to promote their agenda, examines the line between hate speech and free speech, provides an overview of relevant legislation and voluntary industry codes, and suggests ways in which to safeguard children and teens. It is also the place to find seminal articles and the latest reports and surveys on the above issues. Most definitions of hate focus on the ways in which hate-mongers see entire groups of people as the "Other."

For example, U.S.-based Tolerance.org argues that "All hate groups have beliefs or practices that attack or malign an entire class of people, typically for their immutable characteristics." Raymond A. Franklin, author of The Hate Directory, focuses on groups that "advocate violence against, separation from, defamation of, deception about, or hostility towards others based on race, religion, ethnicity, gender, or sexual orientation." Canadian communications scholar Karim Karim points out that the "Other" is one of a number of human archetypes common to all cultures. When people transfer their fears and hatred to the "Other," the targeted group becomes less than human. Hate-mongers can then "justify" acts of violence and degradation because they have denied the humanity of their victims.

The line between hate speech and free speech is a thin one, and different countries have different levels of tolerance. The line is even thinner on the Internet, where hateful comments posted lawfully in one country can be read in other countries where they may be deemed unlawful. Many pundits argue that the best response to hate speech is not criminalisation, but more speech. Philosopher Pierre Lévy reminds us that: More and more, on the Web, ideas are being expressed by the people who are thinking them, and not by journalists who are obliged to simplify or caricature debate because of lack of time or incompetence or, even worse, the political powers that be.

The new medium is therefore particularly conducive to the creation of a public space in the classical sense.

Public debate on the early Net indeed proved frustrating for those who tried to argue that the Holocaust did not occur, or that certain racial groups were inferior. The interactive nature of Usenet newsgroups ensured that false claims were challenged by healthy and vigorous debate. As a result, hate-mongers soon retreated into less interactive areas of cyberspace. Ironically, the free speech environment that characterised discussion forums in the late 1980s and early 1990s made many Internet service providers (ISPs) uncomfortable.

CompuServe was one of the first ISPs to be confronted with a vigorous debate about hate, when a revisionist began to pepper an online discussion with racist comments. The forum soon became one of the most frequently visited on CompuServe. However, the discussion ended when CompuServe created its acceptable use policy, which prohibited people from posting racist or offensive comments. It is now standard practice for ISPs to require online users to adhere to acceptable use policies. Hate-mongers also learned a lesson about the perils of free speech. Canadian Ken McVay, founder of the Nizkor Project, has spent over a decade attempting to engage hate-monger Ernst Zundel in an online discussion.

Web Sites

Web sites also help groups identify potential recruits who can be brought into the hate community through private chat rooms and e-mail, well away from the public eye. However, many activists suggest that the public nature of the Web still works against hate-mongers because their activities can be monitored and brought into the public domain. David Goldman, creator of the now defunct site Hatewatch (the first major site dedicated to tracking the activities of online hate groups) argues:

From the beginning, these organisations' self-proclaimed desire to create a digital "white revolution" was carefully monitored and documented by civil rights organisations, Hatewatch among them. The standard and often repeated quote was the "Internet is the greatest thing to happen to hate." Much to our joy it has in fact been one of the worst. Early fears that the unrestricted nature of online speech would provide haters with an effective recruitment tool appear to be unfounded. The number of hate sites on the Web are increasing day-by day. There is no evidence that the presence of these sites has led to an increase in the number of people who belong to hate groups

Nonetheless, hate groups continue to refine their online strategies.A number of sites encourage their visitors to hack anti-hate Web sites and crash the server or replace the content with hateful messages. For example, hacker Doctor Nuker broke into the American Israel Public Affairs Committee Web site in 2002 and posted anti-Semitic comments on the home page.In another incident, a hate-monger redirected Web traffic so that surfers looking for German government pages were automatically rerouted to pages containing Nazi propaganda. A growing number of countries, including France and Australia, are beginning to exert jurisdiction over online speech in an attempt to curtail hate activities. For example, a French court ordered California-based Yahoo.com to block the auction of Nazi paraphernalia in 2003.

Online Hate

Accordingly, although racist and hateful comments are offensive to the vast majority of people, they are not necessarily illegal. In many developed countries there are laws to prohibit some forms of hate speech. For example let us look at federal law system of Canada which prohibits forms of hate speech. The Canadian Criminal Code provisions are intended to prohibit the public distribution of hate propaganda. Private speech is not covered by the provisions. For example, "advocating genocide" includes publicly arguing that members of an identifiable group should be killed. Wilfully promoting hatred can only be committed by communicating statements other than in a private conversation. And inciting hatred is only prohibited if statements are communicated in a public place. Online communications that advocate genocide or wilfully promote or incite hatred are likely to fall within the provisions because the Internet is a public network.

Under section 320.1 of the Criminal Code, a judge has the authority to order the removal of hate propaganda from a computer system that is available to the public. Such authority extends to all computer systems located within Canada. Section 2 of the Canadian Charter of Rights and Freedoms guarantees freedom of thought, belief, opinion and expression to all Canadians. However, all Charter rights are subject to reasonable limits that can be demonstrably justified in a free and democratic society. In 1990, the Supreme Court of Canada considered whether or not section 319(2) of the Criminal Code (the crime of wilfully promoting hatred) violates our constitutional right to freedom of expression, in the Keegstra case. James Keegstra was an Alberta high-school teacher who taught his students that the Holocaust did not occur and was part of a Jewish conspiracy. The Court held that, although section 319(2) does limit free speech, it is a reasonable limit consistent with a democratic society, and is therefore constitutional.

In January 2002, the Canadian Human Rights Tribunal ordered Ernst Zundel to cease and desist from publishing hate messages on the Zundelsite because his writings violate section 13. However, the Zundelsite continues to post hateful messages because it is located in the United States and is, therefore, outside the jurisdiction of the Canadian tribunal. Regulations under the Broadcasting Act prohibit any licensee from broadcasting or distributing programming that contains abusive comments about individuals or groups - comments that would expose an individual, group, or class of individuals to hatred or contempt on discriminatory grounds.

These regulations apply to radio, specialty services, broadcast television and pay television. However, as it now stands, Internet-based communications do not readily fit the definition of "broadcasting." Under the Immigration Act, customs officials have the authority to stop hate material from entering Canada, and to refuse entry to individual hate-mongers. Bigotry and hatred thrive on ignorance, fear, false information and half-truths. But if readers are able to deconstruct any messages of hate that come their way, much of the messages' power is reduced.

General Features

Capitalise on Paranoia

Conspiracy theories abound on hate sites, which often blame the groups they target for any number of social, economic or political problems. Such theories rely on their readers' ignorance, plus invented "evidence," to back up their claims. One of the most infamous conspiracy theories is contained in the Protocols of the Elders of Zion. The book was written by agents of the Russian czar at the end of the 19th century, and falsely "documents" the existence of a Jewish conspiracy to take over the world. Although such a theory has been thoroughly debunked, hate-mongers continue to invoke the Protocols.

Suggest Sanction from Above

Hate sites often make use of scriptural references, religious writings and holy tracts to give the impression that their claims are sanctified by moral righteousness and guided by a higher power. For example, the site God Hates Fags portrays gays and lesbians in a hateful and demeaning way. Embedded in its homophobic rhetoric are scriptural references to support the position that God has "given up" on gay persons.

Exploit Fear of Armageddon

Hate groups take advantage of people's fears of social and economic uncertainty by blaming the woes of modern society on the particular group they target. Canadian sites like National Skinhead Front, CFAR and the Canadian Heritage Alliance focus on the "dangers" of immigration and the need to return to a "traditional European way of life."

General Strategies

Racialism

White power and white supremacy sites typically deny that they are racist organisations. Instead, they focus on the need to protect white people from assimilation and/ or direct threats from non-white groups. They call this perspective "racialist" as opposed to racist.

Pseudo-science and intellectualism

Many hate-mongers use pseudo-scientific intellectualised language and incorporate the work of university-based academics to make their views seem more credible.

Historical revisionsim

Holocaust denial is a frequently used strategy. Haters who

"revise" history argue that the Holocaust either did not occur, or was less significant than the historical record indicates. The Zundelsite, for example, houses a collection of revisionist writings, including Zundel's pamphlet Did Six Million Really Die?

Patriotism

A number of hate sites clothe their messages in patriotic language. For example, the High Desert Militia of Southern California includes quotes from Thomas Jefferson and Ben Franklin on their home page, beside the "Patriot's Prayer".

Misinformation

A number of hate groups seek to embed their messages in sites that purport to exist for non-hateful purposes. At first glance, the site martinlutherking.org appears to contain historical information about King and the civil rights movement; however, it in fact promotes racism and anti-Semitism. Similarly, the Canadian Association for Free Expression purports to advocate for civil liberties, but its founder, Paul Fromm, admits that the site was created to promote "conservative discussion especially of race and immigration."

Nationalism

Sites such as the U.S.-based League of the South and the Canadian Heritage Alliance use the language of national pride and heritage to advocate for a return to white, "anglo-Celtic civilisation."

Hate symbols

The hate movement continues to use well-known symbols such as the Nazi swastika and the KKK's burning cross to "brand" its message. However, it is increasingly common for hate groups to co-opt mainstream symbols such as the Celtic cross and pagan runes, re-signifying them as emblems of white supremacy.

White supremacist groups and hate groups depend upon recruitment for survival-and their primary target is often teenagers. In their view, impressionable youth represents the only hope for the future of the "white race." Hate groups concentrate their recruiting efforts primarily in high schools (and, to some extent, in colleges and universities). Traditionally, hate groups have had to approach this group with their message by distributing pamphlets on school grounds and in neighbourhood mailboxes. But these tactics are not always successful: too many adults (principals, teachers and parents) are able to intervene to protect the kids. But the Internet seems tailor-made for reaching disaffected young people: teenagers spend far more time on it than their parents do, and many teens consider the virtual world of the web their "home away from home."

Hatemongers now target young people directly, through hate "music" and special web sites. Young people may be susceptible to online racist propaganda because they don't have the experience or facts at hand to refute the lies and myths being fed to them. Lonely, marginalised youth, seeking a sense of identity and belonging, are both the most attractive targets for racists and their most useful tools, once recruited. It's a common belief that youths who join hate groups are mainly poor, uneducated and alienated. Although the Internet is a new way to reach young people, the techniques hatemongers use to attract them are still very traditional. Following are some of the strategies hate groups use to attract young people on the Internet:

– *Music*: Music is a compelling way to influence young people. When kids surf the Net for music, they may chance on sites that sell hate music, or even offer it free for downloading. Such Web sites often also provide links to hate-promoting brochures, pamphlets, newsgroups, chat rooms or Web sites. One of the most popular forms of racist music is "white power" rock 'n' roll-loud and violent, with hostile lyrics that call for the murder of black people, or the start of a racial holy war. Every year in North America, more than 50,000 white power CDs are sold; and journalist Jay Dixit reports that Resistance Records (the largest North American distributor of hate music) was expected to gross more than $1 million (U.S.) in 2001.

– *Games*: Another strategy used to attract young people is white-power versions of popular computer games. Teens may go online looking for the latest cool game, and may find the "hate version" instead. For example, Resistance Records has produced Ethnic Cleansing-a computer game whose object is to kill "subhumans" such as Blacks and Latinos, and their "masters," the Jews, who are portrayed as the personification of evil. Players can choose between dressing as KKK members or skinheads.

– Activities for kids: Some hate sites offer special sections for kids containing games and activities. For example, on the "Creativity for Kids" section of the neo-Nazi World Church of the Creator Web site, children can try their hands at crossword puzzles with racist content. The purpose of the children's section is "to help the young members of the white race understand our fight." Cartoon spokescharacters. Some hate sites use cartoon-like or animated characters, similar to (or identical to) those used in children's media to attract young audiences.

As young people surf the Net in ever-increasing numbers-from schools, libraries and their homes-the risk of them accidentally encountering hate material grows-as does the issue of how to shield them from undesirable online content.

One technical solution often recommended for protecting children is filtering software. Parents and educators can install this software onto their computers, and program it (usually via keywords or phrases) with the type of material they don't want kids to access. The filtering software then "filters out" sites with that kind of content, and blocks the computer browser from going there. Such software is certainly an option for parents of young surfers, who aren't yet adept enough to turn off the filtering software. But as kids get older and more tech-savvy, they can easily find out how to override certain programs. And, of course, filtering software isn't particularly selective: if a parent programs it to block all references to "hate" or "Holocaust," for example, the software will certainly screen out most hate Web sites-but it will also block access to valuable and legitimate resources such as sites dedicated to anti-racism, Jewish culture, war museums, and even discussions of anti-hate legislation.

Another option is to block access to Internet areas that have already been identified as hate sites. The Anti-Defamation League, a U.S. non-profit human-rights group, has developed a product called HateFilter that specifically targets several hundred such Web sites. But regardless of the potential benefits and the drawbacks of such technology, the larger issue is whether to use it to censor young people's access to the Internet in the first place. Filtering software is not a complete solution: hate often comes in subtle forms that filters would not pick up.

The first and best defence for kids on the Internet is always adult guidance. Kids need to know the historical facts about racism and world events, and to talk with parents and teachers about the claims made by hatemongers. Adult involvement is rarer than we might think. MNet's 2001 survey "Young Canadians In A Wired World" revealed that many kids surf the Net at home with little or no parental supervision or awareness.

Seventy per cent of the kids surveyed said their parents "rarely" or "never" ask them about the sites they visit. Hate on the Net is not always obvious: although hard-core sites are easy to detect, some hatemongers use more subtle tactics to attract new blood. They create fun-and-games sites for children and music sites for teens; infiltrate chat-rooms and newsgroups frequented by kids; and even set up sites where children might go for homework assignments.

The most effective long-range strategy for helping young people is to give them lots of information about online hate-as well as the critical thinking skills to decode messages of hate, and read between the lines. A teen might reasonably expect, for instance, a Martin Luther King site to be a place where they could find information on a significant figure in American history. But this Martin Luther King site serves up a potent brew of racism, anti-Semitism and Communist conspiracy theories-all in the guise of historical data. Young people need to understand that the Internet has no gatekeepers and they need to be able to distinguish between such biased prejudicial material, and fair and accurate information.

Privacy Issues

Privacy is a fundamental human right. It underpins human dignity and other values such as freedom of association and freedom of speech. It has become one of the most important human rights of the modern age. Privacy is recognised around the world in diverse regions and cultures. It is protected in the Universal Declaration of Human Rights, the International Covenant on Civil and Political Rights, and in many other international and regional human rights treaties. Nearly every country in the world includes a right of privacy in its constitution.

At a minimum, these provisions include rights of inviolability of the home and secrecy of communications. Most recently written constitutions include specific rights to access and control one's personal information. In many of the countries where privacy is not explicitly recognised in the constitution, the courts have found that right in other provisions. In many countries, international agreements that recognise privacy rights such as the International Covenant on Civil and Political Rights or the European Convention on Human Rights have been adopted into law. Definitions of privacy vary widely according to context and environment.

In many countries, the concept has been fused with data protection, which interprets privacy in terms of management of personal information. Outside this rather strict context, privacy protection is frequently seen as a way of drawing the line at how far society can intrude into a person's affairs. The lack of a single definition should not imply that the issue lacks importance. As one writer observed, "in one sense, all human rights are aspects of the right to privacy." Privacy can be divided into the following separate but related concepts:

- *Information privacy*: which involves the establishment of rules governing the collection and handling of personal data such as credit information, and medical and government records. It is also known as "data protection";
- *Bodily privacy*: which concerns the protection of people's physical selves against invasive procedures such as genetic tests, drug testing and cavity searches;

- *Privacy of communications*: which covers the security and privacy of mail, telephones, e-mail and other forms of communication; and
- *Territorial privacy*: which concerns the setting of limits on intrusion into the domestic and other environments such as the workplace or public space. This includes searches, video surveillance and ID checks.

The World Wide Web is an exciting new marketplace for consumers. It offers easy access not only to a vast array of goods and services, but also to rich sources of information that enable consumers to make better-informed purchasing decisions. It also offers the convenience of shopping from the office or home. This information-rich medium also serves as a source of vast amounts of personal information about consumers. Commercial Web sites collect personal information explicitly through a variety of means, including registration pages, user surveys, and online contests, application forms, and order forms.

Web sites also collect personal information through means that are not obvious to consumers, such as "cookies." The online consumer market is growing exponentially. In early 1997, 51 million adults were already online in the U.S. and Canada, and 73% reported that they had shopped for product information on the World Wide Web. By December 1997, the number of adults online in the U.S. and Canada had climbed to 58 million, and 10 million had actually purchased a product or service online.

Analysts estimate that Internet advertising— which totaled approximately $301 million in 1996—will swell to $4.35 billion by the year 2000. While these figures suggest that the online marketplace is growing rapidly, there are also indications that consumers are wary of participating in it. Surveys have shown that increasing numbers of consumers are concerned about how their personal information is used in the electronic marketplace. In fact, a substantial number of online consumers would rather forego information or products available through the Web than provide a Web site personal information without knowing what the site's information practices are.

According to the results of a March 1998 Business Week survey, consumers not currently using the Internet ranked concerns about the privacy of their personal information and communications as the top reason they have stayed off the Internet. Clearly, consumers care deeply about the privacy and security of their personal information in the online environment and are looking for greater protections. Consumers will continue to distrust online companies and will remain wary of engaging in electronic commerce until meaningful and effective consumer privacy protections are implemented in the online marketplace. If such protections are not implemented, the online marketplace will fail to reach its full potential.

Children represent a large and rapidly growing segment of online consumers and are being actively targeted by commercial Web sites. Children use the Web for a wide variety of activities, including homework, informal learning, browsing, playing games, corresponding with electronic pen pals by e-mail, placing messages on electronic bulletin boards and participating in chat rooms. Among the activities most attractive to children are those that allow them to communicate directly with their peers, for example, chat rooms, bulletin boards and e-mail.

Children are also avid consumers and represent a large and powerful segment of the marketplace. They are estimated to spend billions of dollars a year, and to influence the expenditure of billions more. Their growing presence online, therefore, creates enormous opportunities for marketers to promote their products and services to an eager audience. At the same time, the Web offers an easy way to collect large amounts of detailed marketing data from and about children.

A wide variety of detailed personal information is being collected online from and about children, often without actual notice to or an opportunity for control by parents. This information may be collected from children at various places on a site: when the child is registering for a contest, enrolling in an electronic pen pal program, completing a survey, or playing a game. A child may also reveal such personal information in the course of participating in chat rooms or posting messages on electronic bulletin boards—areas that are publicly accessible to anyone surfing the Web. These practices present unique privacy and safety concerns because of the particular vulnerability of children, the immediacy and ease with which information can be collected from them, and the ability of the online medium to circumvent the traditional gatekeeping role of the parent.

The most potentially serious safety concern is presented by the posting of personal identifying information by and about children—i.e., information that can be used to identify children, such as name, postal or e-mail address—in interactive public areas, like chat rooms and bulletin boards, that are accessible to all online users. These activities enable children to communicate freely with strangers, including adults. The FBI and Justice Department's "Innocent Images" investigation has revealed that online services and bulletin boards are quickly becoming the most powerful resources used by predators to identify and contact children.

Further, anecdotal evidence indicates that many children surfing the Web claim to have experienced problems such as attempted password theft and inappropriate advances by adults in children's chat rooms. Traditionally, parents have instructed children to avoid speaking with strangers. The collecting or posting of personal information in chat rooms and on bulletin boards online runs contrary to that traditional safety message. Children are told by parents not to talk to strangers whom they meet on the street, but they are given a contrary message by Web sites that encourage them to interact with strangers in their homes via the Web.

The dangers in the Web environment are heightened by the fact that children cannot determine whether they are dealing with another child or an adult posing as a child. In addition to these safety issues are privacy concerns raised by commercial Web sites' collection of personal information from children for marketing purposes. As described below, the practice is widespread and includes the collection of personal information from even very young children without any parental involvement or awareness. There is considerable concern about online collection practices that bypass parents, who have traditionally protected children from marketing abuses.

Children generally lack the developmental capacity and judgment to give meaningful consent to the release of personal information to a third party. This is an even greater problem when children are offered an incentive for releasing personal information, or when release of personal information is a prerequisite to registering for a contest, joining a kid's club, or playing a game. In sum, the immediacy and ease with which personal information can be collected from children online, combined with the limited capacity of children to understand fully the potentially serious safety and privacy implications of providing that information, have created deep concerns about current information practices involving children online.

Privacy Protection Principles

Over the past quarter century, government agencies in the United States, Canada, and Europe have studied the manner in which entities collect and use personal information—their "information practices"—and the safeguards required to assure those practices are fair and provide adequate privacy protection. The result has been a series of reports, guidelines, and model codes that represent widely-accepted principles concerning fair information practices. Common to all of these documents are five core principles of privacy protection:

Notice/Awareness: The most fundamental principle is notice. Consumers should be given notice of an entity's information practices before any personal information is collected from them. Without notice, a consumer cannot make an informed decision as to whether and to what extent to disclose personal information. Moreover, three of the other principles discussed below—choice/consent, access/participation, and enforcement/redress—are only meaningful when a consumer has notice of an entity's policies, and his or her rights with respect thereto.

While the scope and content of notice will depend on the entity's substantive information practices, notice of some or all of the following have been recognised as essential to ensuring that consumers are properly informed before divulging personal information:

- identification of the entity collecting the data;
- identification of the uses to which the data will be put;
- identification of any potential recipients of the data;

- the nature of the data collected and the means by which it is collected if not obvious (passively, by means of electronic monitoring, or actively, by asking the consumer to provide the information);
- whether the provision of the requested data is voluntary or required, and the consequences of a refusal to provide the requested information; and
- the steps taken by the data collector to ensure the confidentiality, integrity and quality of the data.

Some information practice codes state that the notice should also identify any available consumer rights, including: any choice respecting the use of the data; whether the consumer has been given a right of access to the data; the ability of the consumer to contest inaccuracies; the availability of redress for violations of the practice code; and how such rights can be exercised. In the Internet context, notice can be accomplished easily by the posting of an information practice disclosure describing an entity's information practices on a company's site on the Web.

To be effective, such a disclosure should be clear and conspicuous, posted in a prominent location, and readily accessible from both the site's home page and any Web page where information is collected from the consumer. It should also be unavoidable and understandable so that it gives consumers meaningful and effective notice of what will happen to the personal information they are asked to divulge.

Choice/Consent: The second widely-accepted core principle of fair information practice is consumer choice or consent. At its simplest, choice means giving consumers options as to how any personal information collected from them may be used. Specifically, choice relates to secondary uses of information—i.e., uses beyond those necessary to complete the contemplated transaction. Such secondary uses can be internal, such as placing the consumer on the collecting company's mailing list in order to market additional products or promotions, or external, such as the transfer of information to third parties. Traditionally, two types of choice/consent regimes have been considered: opt-in or opt-out.

Opt-in regimes require affirmative steps by the consumer to allow the collection and/or use of information; opt-out regimes require affirmative steps to prevent the collection and/or use of such information. The distinction lies in the default rule when no affirmative steps are taken by the consumer. Choice can also involve more than a binary yes/no option. Entities can, and do, allow consumers to tailor the nature of the information they reveal and the uses to which it will be put. Thus, for example, consumers can be provided separate choices as to whether they wish to be on a company's general internal mailing list or a marketing list sold to third parties. In order to be effective, any choice regime should provide a simple and easily-accessible way for consumers to exercise their choice.

In the online environment, choice easily can be exercised by simply clicking a box on the computer screen that indicates a user's decision with respect to the use and/or dissemination of the information being collected. The online environment also presents new possibilities to move beyond the opt-in/opt-out paradigm. For example, consumers could be required to specify their preferences regarding information use before entering a Web site, thus effectively eliminating any need for default rules.

Access/Participation: Access is the third core principle. It refers to an individual's ability both to access data about him or herself —i.e., to view the data in an entity's files—and to contest that data's accuracy and completeness. Both are essential to ensuring that data are accurate and complete. To be meaningful, access must encompass timely and inexpensive access to data, a simple means for contesting inaccurate or incomplete data, a mechanism by which the data collector can verify the information, and the means by which corrections and/or consumer objections can be added to the data file and sent to all data recipients.

Integrity/Security: The fourth widely accepted principle is that data be accurate and secure. To assure data integrity, collectors must take reasonable steps, such as using only reputable sources of data and cross-referencing data against multiple sources, providing consumer access to data, and destroying untimely data or converting it to anonymous form. Security involves both managerial and technical measures to protect against loss and the unauthorised access, destruction, use, or disclosure of the data.

Managerial measures include internal organisational measures that limit access to data and ensure that those individuals with access do not utilise the data for unauthorised purposes. Technical security measures to prevent unauthorised access include encryption in the transmission and storage of data; limits on access through use of passwords; and the storage of data on secure servers or computers that are inaccessible by modem.

Enforcement/Redress: It is generally agreed that the core principles of privacy protection can only be effective if there is a mechanism in place to enforce them. Absent an enforcement and redress mechanism, a fair information practice code is merely suggestive rather than prescriptive, and does not ensure compliance with core fair information practice principles. Among the alternative enforcement approaches are industry self-regulation; legislation that would create private remedies for consumers; and/or regulatory schemes enforceable through civil and criminal sanctions.

Self-Regulation: To be effective, self-regulatory regimes should include both mechanisms to ensure compliance (enforcement) and appropriate means of recourse by injured parties (redress). Mechanisms to ensure compliance include making acceptance of and compliance with a code of fair information practices a condition of membership in an industry association; external audits to verify compliance; and certification of entities that have adopted and comply with the code at issue.

A self-regulatory regime with many of these principles has recently been adopted by the individual reference services industry. Appropriate means of individual redress include, at a minimum, institutional mechanisms to ensure that consumers have a simple and effective way to have their concerns addressed. Thus, a self-regulatory system should provide a means to investigate complaints from individual consumers and ensure that consumers are aware of how to access such a system. If the self-regulatory code has been breached, consumers should have a remedy for the violation. Such a remedy can include both the righting of the wrong (e.g., correction of any misinformation, cessation of unfair practices) and compensation for any harm suffered by the consumer. Monetary sanctions would serve both to compensate the victim of unfair practices and as an incentive for industry compliance. Industry codes can provide for alternative dispute resolution mechanisms to provide appropriate compensation.

Private Remedies: A statutory scheme could create private rights of action for consumers harmed by an entity's unfair information practices. Several of the major information practice codes, including the seminal 1973 HEW Report, call for implementing legislation. The creation of private remedies would help create strong incentives for entities to adopt and implement fair information practices and ensure compensation for individuals harmed by misuse of their personal information. Important questions would need to be addressed in such legislation, e.g., the definition of unfair information practices; the availability of compensatory, liquidated and/or punitive damages; and the elements of any such cause of action.

Government Enforcement: Finally, government enforcement of fair information practices, by means of civil or criminal penalties, is a third means of enforcement. Fair information practice codes have called for some government enforcement, leaving open the question of the scope and extent of such powers. Whether enforcement is civil or criminal likely will depend on the nature of the data at issue and the violation committed.

The fair information practice codes are, however, applicable to parents, in light of the special status that children generally have been accorded under the law. This status as a special, vulnerable group is premised on the belief that children lack the analytical abilities and judgment of adults. It is evidenced by an array of federal and state laws that protect children, including those that ban sales of tobacco and alcohol to minors, prohibit child pornography, require parental consent for medical procedures, and make contracts with children voidable. In the specific arenas of marketing and privacy rights, moreover, several federal statutes and regulations recognise both the need for heightened protections for children and the special role that parents play in implementing these protections.

Participation and Integrity Principles

Since parents may not be fully aware of what personal information a site has collected from their child, the access/participation principle is a particularly important one with respect to information collected from children. To provide informed consent to the retention and/or use of information collected from their children, parents need to be given access to the information collected from their children, particularly if any of the information is collected prior to providing notice to the parent.

The principle of integrity, which addresses the accuracy of the data, is also important for children's information. Parents have an interest in assuring that whatever information Web sites collect from children or have otherwise obtained about their children is accurate. This is particularly important in contexts that involve decisions that impact on the child or family, such as educational or health decisions. In addition, since children's information is considered to be a more sensitive type of information, sites should take the same steps identified above to assure that children's data is secure from unauthorised uses or disclosures.

Privacy Protection

There are four major models for privacy protection. Depending on their application, these models can be complementary or contradictory. In most countries reviewed in the survey, several are used simultaneously. In the countries that protect privacy most effectively, all of the models are used together to ensure privacy protection.

Comprehensive laws: In many countries around the world, there is a general law that governs the collection, use and dissemination of personal information by both the public and private sectors. An oversight body then ensures compliance. This is the preferred model for most countries adopting data protection laws and was adopted by the European Union to ensure compliance with its data protection regime. A variation of these laws, which is described as a "co-regulatory model," was adopted in Canada and Australia. Under this approach, industry develops rules for the protection of privacy that are enforced by the industry and overseen by the privacy agency.

Sectoral Laws: Some countries, such as the United States, have avoided enacting general data protection rules in favor of specific sectoral laws governing, for example, video rental records and financial privacy. In such cases, enforcement is achieved through a range of mechanisms. A major drawback with this approach is that it requires that new legislation be introduced with each new technology so protections frequently lag behind. The lack of legal protections for individual's privacy on the Internet in the United States is a striking example of its limitations. There is also the problem of a lack of an oversight agency. In many countries, sectoral laws are used to complement comprehensive legislation by providing more detailed protections for certain categories of information, such as telecommunications, police files or consumer credit records.

Self-Regulation : Data protection can also be achieved, at least in theory, through various forms of self-regulation, in which companies and industry bodies establish codes of practice and engage in self-policing. However, in many countries, especially the United States, these efforts have been disappointing, with little evidence that the aims of the codes are regularly fulfilled. Adequacy and enforcement are the major problem with these approaches.

Industry codes in many countries have tended to provide only weak protections and lack enforcement.

Technology-based Privacy : With the recent development of commercially available technology-based systems, privacy protection has also moved into the hands of individual users. Users of the Internet and of some physical applications can employ a range of programs and systems that provide varying degrees of privacy and security of communications. These include encryption, anonymous remailers, proxy servers and digital cash. Users should be aware that not all tools effectively protect privacy. Some are poorly designed while others may be designed to facilitate law enforcement access.

Right to Privacy: The recognition of privacy is deeply rooted in history. There is recognition of privacy in the Qur'an and in the sayings of Mohammed. The Bible has numerous references to privacy. Jewish law has long recognised the concept of being free from being watched. There were also protections in classical Greece and ancient China. Legal protections have existed in Western countries for hundreds of years. In 1361, the Justices of the Peace Act in England provided for the arrest of peeping toms and eavesdroppers.

In 1765, British Lord Camden, striking down a warrant to enter a house and seize papers wrote, "We can safely say there is no law in this country to justify the defendants in what they have done; if there was, it would destroy all the comforts of society, for papers are often the dearest property any man can have." Parliamentarian William Pitt wrote, "The poorest man may in his cottage bid defiance to all the force of the Crown. It may be frail; its roof may shake; the wind may blow through it; the storms may enter; the rain may enter - but the King of England cannot enter; all his forces dare not cross the threshold of the ruined tenement."

In 1776, the Swedish Parliament enacted the Access to Public Records Act that required that all government-held information be used for legitimate purposes. France prohibited the publication of private facts and set stiff fines for violators in 1858. The Norwegian Criminal Code prohibited the publication of information relating to "personal or domestic affairs" in 1889. The modern privacy benchmark at an international level can be found in the 1948 Universal Declaration of Human Rights, which specifically protects territorial and communications privacy. Article 12 states: No one should be subjected to arbitrary interference with his privacy, family, home or correspondence, nor to attacks on his honour or reputation.

Everyone has the right to the protection of the law against such interferences or attacks. Numerous international human rights treaties specifically recognise privacy as a right. The International Covenant on Civil and Political Rights (ICCPR), Article 17, the United Nations Convention on Migrant Workers, Article 14, and the UN Convention on Protection of the Child, Article 16 adopt the same language. On the regional level, various treaties make these rights legally enforceable. Article 8 of the European Convention for the Protection of Human Rights and Fundamental Freedoms 1950 states:

- Everyone has the right to respect for his private and family life, his home and his correspondence.
- There shall be no interference by a public authority with the exercise of this right except as in accordance with the law and is necessary in a democratic society in the interests of national security, public safety or the economic well-being of the country, for the prevention of disorder or crime, for the protection of health of morals, or for the protection of the rights and freedoms of others.

The Convention created the European Commission of Human Rights and the European Court of Human Rights to oversee enforcement. Both have been active in the enforcement of privacy rights and have consistently viewed Article 8's protections expansively and interpreted the restrictions narrowly. The Commission found in 1976: For numerous Anglo-Saxon and French authors, the right to respect "private life" is the right to privacy, the right to live, as far as one wishes, protected from publicity. In the opinion of the Commission, however, the right to respect for private life does not end there. It comprises also, to a certain degree, the right to establish and develop relationships with other human beings, especially in the emotional field for the development and fulfillment of one's own personality.

The Court has reviewed member states' laws and imposed sanctions on numerous countries for failing to regulate wiretapping by governments and private individuals. It has also reviewed cases of individuals' access to their personal information in government files to ensure that adequate procedures exist. It has expanded the protections of Article 8 beyond government actions to those of private persons where it appears that the government should have prohibited those actions. Article 11 of the American Convention on Human Rights sets out the right to privacy in terms similar to the Universal Declaration. In 1965, the Organisation of American States proclaimed the American Declaration of the Rights and Duties of Man, which called for the protection of numerous human rights, including privacy. The Inter-American Court of Human Rights has begun to address privacy issues in its cases.

Protection of Data

Interest in the right of privacy increased in the 1960s and

1970s with the advent of information technology. The surveillance potential of powerful computer systems prompted demands for specific rules governing the collection and handling of personal information. The genesis of modern legislation in this area can be traced to the first data protection law in the world enacted in the Land of Hesse in Germany in 1970. This was followed by national laws in Sweden, the United States, Germany, and France. Two crucial international instruments evolved from these laws. The Council of Europe's 1981 Convention for the Protection of Individuals with regard to the Automatic Processing of Personal Data and the Organisation for Economic Cooperation and Development's (OECD) Guidelines Governing the Protection of Privacy and Transborder Data Flows of Personal Data set out specific rules covering the handling of electronic data. These rules describe personal information as data that are afforded protection at every step from collection to storage and dissemination.

The expression of data protection in various declarations and laws varies. All require that personal information must be:

- obtained fairly and lawfully;
- used only for the original specified purpose;
- adequate, relevant and not excessive to purpose;
- accurate and up to date;
- accessible to the subject;
- kept secure; and
- destroyed after its purpose is completed.

These two agreements have had a profound effect on the enactment of laws around the world. Nearly thirty countries have signed the COE convention and several others are planning to do so shortly. There are three major reasons for the movement towards comprehensive privacy and data protection laws. Many countries are adopting these laws for one or more reasons.

1. To remedy past injustices. Many countries, especially in Central Europe, South America and South Africa, are adopting laws to remedy privacy violations that occurred under previous authoritarian regimes.

2. To promote electronic commerce. Many countries, especially in Asia, have developed or are currently developing laws in an effort to promote electronic commerce. These countries recognise that consumers are uneasy with the increased availability of their personal data, particularly with new means of identification and forms of transactions. These countries recognise consumers are uneasy with their personal information being sent worldwide. Privacy laws are being introduced as part of a package of laws intended to facilitate electronic commerce by setting up uniform rules.

3. To ensure laws are consistent with Pan-European laws. Most countries in Central and Eastern Europe are adopting new laws based on the Council of Europe Convention and the European Union Data Protection Directive. Many of these countries hope to join the European Union in the near future. Countries in other regions are adopting new laws or updating older laws to ensure that trade will not be affected by the requirements of the European Union Directive.

In 1995, the European Union enacted the Data Protection Directive in order to harmonise member states' laws in providing consistent levels of protections for citizens and ensuring the free flow of personal data within the European Union. The directive sets a baseline common level of privacy that not only reinforces current data protection law, but also establishes a range of new rights. It applies to the processing of personal information in electronic and manual files. A key concept in the European data protection model is "enforceability." Data subjects have rights established in explicit rules. Every European Union country has a data protection commissioner or agency that enforces the rules. It is expected that the countries with which Europe does business will need to provide a similar level of oversight.

The basic principles established by the Directive are: the right to know where the data originated; the right to have inaccurate data rectified; a right of recourse in the event of unlawful processing; and the right to withhold permission to use data in some circumstances. For example, individuals have the right to opt-out free of charge from being sent direct marketing material. The Directive contains strengthened protections over the use of sensitive personal data relating, for example, to health, sex life or religious or philosophical beliefs. In the future, the commercial and government use of such information will generally require "explicit and unambiguous" consent of the data subject.

The 1995 Directive imposes an obligation on member states to ensure that the personal information relating to European citizens has the same level of protection when it is exported to, and processed in, countries outside the European Union. This requirement has resulted in growing pressure outside Europe for the passage of privacy laws. Those countries that refuse to adopt adequate privacy laws may find themselves unable to conduct certain types of information flows with Europe, particularly if they involve sensitive data. In 1997, the European Union supplemented the 1995 directive by introducing the Telecommunications Privacy Directive. This directive established specific protections covering telephone, digital television, mobile networks and other telecommunications systems. It imposed wide-ranging obligations on carriers and service providers to ensure the privacy of users' communications, including Internet-related activities. It covered areas that, until then, had fallen between the cracks of data protection laws.

Access to billing data was severely restricted, as was marketing activity. Caller ID technology was required to incorporate an option for per-line blocking of number transmission. Information collected in the delivery of a communication was required to be purged once the call was completed. An essential aspect of any privacy protection regime is oversight. In most countries with an omnibus data protection or privacy act, there is an official or agency that oversees enforcement of the act. The powers of these officials, Commissioner, Ombudsman or Registrar, vary widely by country.Several countries including Germany and Canada also have officials or offices on a state or provincial level.

Under Article 28 of the European Union Data Protection Directive, all European Union countries must have an independent enforcement body. Under the Directive, these agencies are given considerable power: governments must consult the body when the government draws up legislation relating to the processing of personal information; the bodies also have the power to conduct investigations and have a right to access information relevant to their investigations; impose remedies such as ordering the destruction of information or ban processing, and start legal proceedings, hear complaints and issue reports. The official is also generally responsible for public education and international liaison in data protection and data transfer.

Many authorities also maintain the register of data controllers and databases. They must approve licensing for data controllers. Several countries that do not have a comprehensive act still have a commissioner. A major power of these officials is to focus public attention on problem areas, even when they do not have any authority to fix the problem. They can do this by promoting codes of practice and encouraging industry associations to adopt them. They also can use their annual reports to point out problems. For example, in Canada, the Federal Privacy Commissioner announced in his 2000 report the existence of an extensive database maintained by the federal government. Once the issue became public, the Ministry disbanded the database. In several countries, this official also serves as the enforcer of the jurisdiction's Freedom of Information Act. These include Hungary, Estonia, Thailand and the United Kingdom.On the sub-national level, many of the German Lund Commissioners have recently been given the power of information commissioner, and most of the Canadian provincial agencies handle both data protection and freedom of information.

A major problem with many agencies around the world is a lack of resources to adequately conduct oversight and enforcement. Many are burdened with licensing systems, which use much of their resources. Others have large backlogs of complaints or are unable to conduct significant number of investigations. Many that started out with adequate funding find their budgets cut a few years later. Independence is also a problem. In many countries, the agency is under the control of the political arm of the government or part of the Ministry of Justice and lacks the power or will to advance privacy or criticise privacy invasive proposals.

In Japan and Thailand, the oversight agency is under the control of the Prime Minister's Office. In Thailand, the director was transferred in 2000 after conflicts with the Prime Minister's Office. In 2001, Slovenia amended its Data Protection Act in order to establish an independent supervisory authority and thereby ensure compliance with the Data Protection Directive. Finally, in some countries that do not have a separate office, the role of investigating and enforcing the laws is done by a human rights ombudsman or by a parliamentary official. Most data protection laws include restrictions on the transfer of information to third countries unless the information is protected in the destination country.

For example, Article 12 of the Council of Europe's 1981 Convention places restrictions on the transborder flows of personal data. Similarly, Article 25 of the European Directive imposes an obligation on member States to ensure that any personal information relating to European citizens is protected by law when it is exported to, and processed in, countries outside Europe. It states: The Member States shall provide that the transfer to a third country of personal data which are undergoing processing or are intended for processing after transfer may take place only if the third country in question ensures an adequate level of protection. This requirement has resulted in growing pressure outside Europe for the passage of strong data protection laws. Those countries that refuse to adopt meaningful privacy laws may find themselves unable to conduct certain types of information flows with Europe, particularly if they involve sensitive data.

Determination of a third country's system for protecting privacy is made by the European Commission. The overarching principle in this determination process is that the level of protection in the receiving country must be "adequate" rather than "equivalent." Therefore, a reasonably high standard of protection is expected from the third party, although the precise dictates of the Directive need not be followed. On July 26, 2000, the European Commission ruled that both Switzerland and Hungary provide "adequate" protection for personal information and therefore that all transfers of personal data to these countries could continue.

8

Influence of Media on New Generation

Toward the end of the 20 century, as technology revolutionised communication, the mass audience was also breaking up into special interest groups or market segments. Alvin Toffler saw the "crack-up of the industrial mass society" and the split of the "mass market" into "ever-multiplying, ever changing sets of mini-markets that demand a continually expanding range of options, models, types, sizes, colours and customisations." The new communications media saw the rise of special publications; some taking the form of newsletters sent out to far-flung communities, catering to small groups bound by common issues and interests. When video recorders enabled on-demand programmes and movies, television networks lost their power to dictate and synchronise viewing hours.

Cable increased programme choices for the viewing audience and citizen band radio promoted greater interaction among listeners. The computer allowed communication and information flows to cut through time zones and to undermine geography as an indicator of one's location or address. The Internet has carried any material carried in traditional communication formats while creating original cyber news channels. These advances have required the development of new skills and prodded the rise of a new form of literacy in the field of communication-knowing where to find what kind of information.

As the sources of information have proliferated, access has involved special skills that the public has had to learn. These skills enable the individual to become his own gatekeeper of the news, seeking information as the need arises. All of the above have wrenched primary control over the flow of news from the elite news organisations that have for so long determined the course of newsgathering and dissemination. Much has been said about the decline of the news audience in the US. In 1980, Toffler traced the statistics showing the circulation losses of leading newspapers across the nation. Between 1970 and 1977, despite a 14 million rise in US population, the combined aggregate circulation of the remaining top twenty-five magazines dropped by 4 million.

The decline in newspaper readership was matched by growth in radio and cable television, media that have traditionally rooted its function and purpose in entertainment. Neil Postman listed the elements of television news-"the good looks and amiability of the cast, their pleasant banter, the exciting music that opens and closes the show, the vivid film footage, the attractive commercials", rendering news as a diversion and distraction, as what has been called 'info-tainment.' The decline of newspapers may be linked to the diminished public engagement and public interest in politics.

William Greider noted the decrease of voting in presidential elections in the US since 1960, the narrow base of votes for representatives, and the minority votes that have decided election outcomes in the US Congress. Polls have also shown that after 1990, three in four Americans expressed dissatisfaction with the outcomes in congressional elections, even when their candidates won. The world pictured in much of the news suggests that citizen engagement won't make a difference in improving the state of things. At the same time, in many developed societies of the West, populations are becoming more educated than their predecessors, who presume post-graduate degrees as a requirement for most careers. This public constitutes a more discerning market and more critical users of the news.

It is not surprising then that individuals choose to connect with the outside world on their own, creating conversing communities as they enter chat rooms and click onto Web sites. Through the Internet and the global transmission of live television, the news comes to them real-time, enjoying virtually the same access available to experts, government leaders and journalists. Some consumers of news possess so much more expertise about a range of subjects-a background that equips them to analyse events and issues for themselves. These people exist side by side the uncritical mass that are satisfied with pap and pulp in the media. The dual audience expects and demands opposing values in the news.

The Internet allows the people to become their own information and news provider. The global trend toward democratisation continues to place the institution of the press at the heart of critical social and political concerns. Democracy highlights the importance of information in a society and continued learning and education as a feature of public life. The press has been ideally positioned to provide information that citizens need to know in order to participate in public affairs. The news media are instruments of open debate and discussion in society, engaging citizens in a continuing exchange of ideas about the issues of the times. Quite simply, a free press expands freedom and strengthens democracy.

In different parts of the world, technology has eased the political shift toward democratisation. Indonesia opened up its society to satellite technology and the availability of news and programmes from all over the world was slowly changing the public mind set in the country, even before the breakdown of Suharto's authoritarian regime. Later, the Internet quickened the pace of information dissemination among activists who challenged Suharto's long-standing rule. In the Philippines, the SMS or text-message system through cell phones enhanced the mobilisation of mass rallies protesting the corruption of the Estrada government. Communication technology has also dramatically recast the character of politics.

In the US, studies have shown how television has changed the style of political campaigns and the manner by which the voter makes an electoral choice. The visual media in America politics has made possible a greater degree of manipulation of candidates' images. In a study of the impact of television on American presidential elections, Grossman notes that television allows people direct access to political figures and events. But it also emphasises "personality, visual image and emotion rather than on ideas, issues, and reason." In less developed democracies like the Philippines, television has pressed political parties to field candidates from show business or the media. In these two different environments, the use of television media has less to do with journalism than with the manufacture of media images and impressions.

On another level, Grossman notes the development of the "electronic republic" forming in America: "a democratic system that is vastly increasing the people's day-to-day influence on the decisions of the state." The growth of telecommunications media involves citizens more directly in their own governance. This is true even in developing societies. In the Philippines, instant polls conducted by TV or radio programmes engage their viewers by asking them to text or call in their votes on questions related to controversial policy issues. There is little point to such communication without an educated and engaged citizenry. However, it can also be said that such communication makes it possible to form and sustain such a public. Otherwise, technology only facilitates the tyranny of the ignorant majority.

Compared to developing democracies, relatively higher levels of information literacy may be found in the mainstream population of industrial societies. Citizens in these countries may have more education in general to make worthy interventions. However, where there is less development and less resources, the public may remain as the misguided and misdirected mass. By providing the means for continuing public information and education, the press helps society to achieve its goals.

Embedded in all democratic theory is the principle of the free market. Underlying the development of free press enterprise is the commercial drive that operates all kinds of business. In search of a media audience, the press has been driven by the profit issue and the need to make money. In this new age of communication, the practice and business of journalism involves the pursuit of an audience. News organisations and news outlets need to claim an audience share to attract advertisers. Advertising revenue provides media profits.

Commercialisation has shaped the news product, imposing certain criteria based on popular appeal. Although the concept of 'news-worthiness' has always included relevance and significance, the press often excludes important and compelling news. Applied in different newsrooms, these values evolve news packages that are as different from each other in style and substance- the tabloids co-exist with high-minded broadsheets, the info-tainment segments hold their time against serious newscasting. But they all still adhere to certain traditional criteria of what makes 'news.' As such, news may become limited in scope and in subject and limited by space and time, conditions that in a way impose a certain predictability to the news.

How often have we heard people say that they are tired of reading about the same things? After a while, the scandals, the celebrities and controversies all seem the same, echoing elements from similar incidents in the past. Was it Thoreau who said he had no need to know about yet another fire, murder or accident? These days, can we also say that we have not yet seen all there is to know about scandal and scalawags, celebrities and the lives of the rich and famous? The mandate of the mass markets has evolved a news culture more likely to entertain than educate, to distract rather than instruct the public. In highly productive economies in the West, popular demand for more and more entertainment and recreation presses on editorial policies. In the political field, political campaigns have made use of entertainment vehicles and advertising formats to get their message across or to attract the electorate.

In the US, studies have shown the impact of commerce on people's perceptions about candidates. A study of the role of political advertising and televised news showed that people responded more to the stimulus of advertising messages that they did to the message in the news. In emerging democracies as in established democracies, news organisations have adjusted to the reality and merged entertainment and information goals. Cases have shown how commercialisation has marginalised news and information that is relevant to political discourse.

The situation confronts the press with a critical challenge to revise and reinvent news practice to address change. Its failure to address the challenge of change wastes historic opportunity and the unique resources unleashed in the information age to create a learning society. The same failure can lead to a press diminished in significance and relevance. With the growth of competition, popularisation has also resulted in a news style designed to attract more people, to pander to the public taste for the sensational and exciting. The tabloid culture has dominated and eroded news values.

Editorial decisions so often ignore what is significant and relevant because these are more difficult to make interesting and appealing. The greatest human stories are processes which aren't reported well. The narrow focus on events has allowed the process of environmental deterioration to go unreported. Not until the event of an environmental disaster does it make it as news, and by then it is too late. Events reporting can lead reporters to miss the context, the connections that make reality more understandable.

People complain that staple of bad news can be disheartening, building up a sense of helplessness that may disable a community from doing anything to address their problems. The press may exaggerate its adversarial stance in reporting on government, concentrating on failures and excluding the successes. This could engender continuing public frustration. This kind of outlook does not foster the community spirit that feeds democracy. Journalism serves citizens.

Journalism must draw citizen attention to that which is significant and meaningful, to information that they need to know, although they may not necessarily be conscious of the need. It has been easier to give the public what is easy for them to appreciate, such as distracting and entertaining news. It is much more difficult to hold their attention with the accounts that try to make sense of developments affecting their lives. Given a measure of information literacy for the greater numbers, the press must help this public find meaning in the mass of information that is at hand. The Internet allows the public direct access to so much government information.

Even though the Internet will make it easier to get the information, the public will still face the same daunting challenge of sorting through it. The need for adjustment on the part of journalists if the press is to remain as the dominant source of news and information. Journalists need to be as literate in technology but at the same time, they must safeguard its strengths, retain their ability to get to the sources and to evaluate the information they are given, and maintain the facility to connect different kinds of knowledge so these can make larger sense for those who only see part of it.

Finally, journalists must continue to do what they have always done for the public, providing interesting accounts of the day's events, explaining and synthesising different developments of significance, while observing the requirements of fairness and ethics. Inherent in journalism-online or on traditional media-is the purpose of community; meaning a community of free men and women who have sovereign will. They need to be connected with a shared fund of information that serves for them a common reference with which to think on the issues of the day and to weigh their options as citizens. Returning to the roots of journalism, the advocates of public or civic journalism urge the restoration of the community of citizens in the centre of press concerns.

The public dialogue and civic involvement of members a community forms "the civic capital" that is the basis of press enterprise. Without it, there is no real point to journalism. Journalism should replenish these civic resources and build up more public life. A public is something more than a market for information, an audience for spectacle, or a pollster's random sample. Publics are formed when we turn from our private and separate affairs to face common problems, and to face each other in dialogue and discussion. Information technology could draw away community members from the public forum, making them feel self-sufficient in their cocoons of selected news and information.

Journalists need to understand how these trends can be inimical to democratic society and craft practice that will rebuild their connections with the community and to strengthen public life. The new technologies of information and communications (NTIC) have revolutionised the day-to-day work of journalists and they provide new opportunities for journalists to work better, more efficiently and more professionally. Reporters and media professionals should play a key role in the development of the information society.

If the information society is truly about providing the knowledge, skills and services that will enrich peoples' lives and bolster democratic participation at large, then journalists must have access to new technologies that will strengthen their professional capacity to ensure reliable, quality, and accurate information for public consumption—whatever the mode of its dissemination. But will this happen? In spite of great optimism fostered a decade ago when information change began to drive the process of globalisation, the reality for journalists in many parts of the world is that they are among those most affected by the digital divide.

Public confidence will not grow unless more is done to guarantee people's rights and to engage them in the debate over the consequences of change. Unable to tune in and log on to the advantages of the information revolution, journalists in developing countries face enormous challenges in their social and professional lives. Their technologically deprived conditions make them the second and third class citizens of the world of journalism and their mission to inform, particularly in the least developed countries, suffers as a result.

Television and Young Generation

Television is the dominant medium for young people-and adults-around the world. From the mid-1980s to the mid-1990s, the number of television channels, household television sets and hours spent watching television more than doubled. There are now approximately 250 television sets per thousand inhabitants in the world-far more than the number of telephones. Satellite television reaches all continents, offering increasing numbers of channels targeting specific market segments, including young viewers.

In the late 1990s, some 50 television channels directed specifically to children were launched, several of which have had enormous international success. However, this has caused national television services in many areas to cut back their own production of children's programmes. As the graphs illustrate, weekly television viewing far surpasses radio listening in nearly every region, and dwarfs newspaper and internet use. Average daily use of television among those school-age children around the world with access ranges from between 1.5 hours to more than four hours; many of these same children will rarely read a book.

The prominence of television in young people's daily lives makes it one of their major information sources about the world around them. The prevalence of television viewing among young people raises serious concerns about recent national and global trends in the television industry. The rampant consolidation of commercial media has meant the dominance of only a handful of large and powerful companies. In industrialised countries, there have been recent outcries over rising levels of aggression, obesity, substance abuse, eating disorders and unsafe sexual behaviour among youth, increasingly attributed to commercial media aimed at children and youth.

In developing countries, where resources limit domestic productions, a majority of programmes for children and youth are imported. Unfortunately, much of the content contains characters and messages that, at best, are simply not relevant to local cultures, and at worst convey violent images and mass marketing messages. Plus, public broadcasters that have traditionally produced some of the best-quality children's media have had to reduce their youth programming in the face of funding cuts and growing competition from private channels. Clearly the case for media pluralism, i.e., access to media that effectively communicates and supplies relevant content, applies to children and young people as well.

Use of Radio

After television viewing, listening to the radio is the next most popular activity among children and young people worldwide. Actual listening rates among the young vary greatly, however, depending on the quality of national broadcasting and the availability of private alternatives. In many countries, there has been a boom among young people in radio listening over the past decade, the result of the emergence of dozens of private radio stations. This is particularly the case in Africa and the former Soviet bloc countries. Most young people tune in to the radio primarily for music and entertainment.

However, some local radio stations have been very successful in attracting and informing more socially active segments of the population, young and old alike. A good example is the ANEM network of independent radio stations in the former Yugoslavia. It has become a major source of diverse information and entertainment for youth interested in social life. In some countries, listening to the largely political fare of public international radio broadcasters-the BBC, VOA, Deutsche Welle and Radio France Internationale, among them-remains surprisingly high among young people. According to 2003 surveys, 16 percent of young people 15 to 19 listened to international radio in Albania, 12 percent in Bangladesh, 21 percent in Nigeria and 26 percent in urban Haiti. These relatively high listening rates testify to young people's interest in political and social events, and reflect the need for high-quality information, still lacking in many countries.

Use of Computers

The internet has been gaining popularity among young people, though at a much slower pace than television and radio. In spite of significant differences among the developed and developing world, the use of computers and the internet is rising steadily, fastest among young men. That there are so many more computer-literate young people than adults indicates the younger generation's greater interest in and aptitude for technological advances. Around the world, young users are increasingly turning to the internet as a source of information, communication, socialising and entertainment.

At the same time, web access is the source of the greatest divide, both between countries (internet use in industrialised countries far outpaces use in the developing world), and within countries (internet use concentrated among wealthier and better-educated urban youth). Nevertheless, even in countries where internet and computer use is low, young people actively seek access whenever possible, most often in internet cafes. Young people are enthusiastic about the internet because, more than any other medium, it helps them establish contact with the outside world and freely seek information.

Perhaps it is 'free' access to information that also accounts for the higher levels of trust young people (and adults as well) often place in information on the web than in information from traditional media. But, the openness of the web and young people's apparent inability to distinguish clearly between content and advertising worries parents and child advocates alike. Young people use the internet primarily for communicating (email and chat rooms); downloading (computer games, software and music); and obtaining information (about education, entertainment, sports, "taboo" topics not addressed by adults, and news that may be censored for political motives).

Print Media

In contrast to the steady rise of other media, in many countries print media have experienced a setback from the role they once played. Several recent developments have served to further decrease the numbers of young readers of print media. In part, this is a result of the improved quantity and quality of information available from television and radio. In industrialised countries, young people are distracted by numerous media choices and technologies. In poorer countries, few youth-oriented publications exist and those that do often have limited circulation or are too expensive for most youth to afford.

In the former Soviet bloc countries, youth press once played a fairly vibrant role and received significant government backing. Since the fall of the Berlin Wall, however, youth press has largely disappeared and has not been replaced by a regular alternative forum for young people. Starting in the early 1990s, newspaper readership levels declined sharply throughout the region, especially in those countries experiencing the greatest economic difficulties. Many publications folded without government subsidies and could not attract sufficient advertisers or subscribers. Those that did survive had to raise their prices, making them unaffordable for many.

Lastly, the distribution system was so badly weakened in many countries that it is now common for newspapers and magazines to arrive in rural areas weeks and months late, if at all. The publications in strongest demand among young people are those that appeal to their specialised interests-comic books and popular specialised magazines on computers, fashion, sports, science, business and music. Many are high quality, with slick and appealing content that cater to young people's interests, yet are often too costly for the average young person (or adult).

In spite of improvements in quantity and quality of media for children and youth around the world over the last decade, there still exists an informational divide both between and within countries. The divide between better-educated, wealthier youth and less-educated, rural youth determines access to, use of and preferences for different types of media. The informational divide takes many different forms. In developing countries, highest overall media use most often occurs among urban, affluent young people. But in some countries, television viewing rates are just as high in rural as in urban areas because of community viewing habits and because of the lack of alternative media.

In industrialised countries, in contrast, media use tends to be highest among lower socio-economic groups because television is inexpensive entertainment. While wealthier young people devote less time to television and video games, they spend more time using computers and print media. Boys tend to access media more than girls, and use audio-visual and digital media more often as well. Yet, in some cultures, the opposite is true because restrictions on girls' activities often keep them at home. For the same reason, boys frequent outdoor places of entertainment more often, such as cinemas, internet cafes and video parlours.

The vast majority of young people in the world do not have access to computers or the internet, mainly due to economic reasons. Buying a computer and securing a web connection are still big investments in many countries. In addition, poor infrastructure puts young people in smaller towns and villages at a disadvantage. Technical problems also discourage wide internet use in some countries and do not allow young people to fully appreciate all the possibilities the web offers. Apart from economic considerations, there are also young people who shy away from the internet because of the prevalence of English-language content, or the absence of content in their own language.

Others are simply not particularly interested or do not fully understand its uses and possibilities. As media options for most children have grown in recent decades, so too have concerns about the quality of media aimed at children. Growing numbers of parents, educators, researchers and policy-makers around the world are alarmed about the lack of quality media for children and young people and the growing availability of low-quality entertainment featuring violence, sexual content, undesirable role models and lack of diversity. There are also serious questions about the short- and long-term effects of this material.

Numerous studies have been done on the effects of media-violence in media in particular-on children. Young people often speak of the power the media has on their lives, and any parent can attest to the impressionable, unquestioning and imitative nature of children. How much the mass media influence children and young people is somewhat debatable, but sociologists and researchers in different regions have observed some of the following adverse effects:

- growing influence of entertainment media on youth style and identity
- decreasing role of traditional sources of influence: family, school, community, religion, etc.
- appeal of individualism and personal, as opposed to collective or societal, achievement
- some confusion in values (misguided sense of right and wrong, of human relations)
- an increasingly blurred line between advertisements and programme content
- distortion of reality and rising expectation gaps
- newfound culture of "glamour" and "celebrity"
- creation of harmful or unrealistic stereotypes; a promotion of intolerance or apathy
- emphasis on the banal and trivial; de-emphasis on education, creativity and culture
- tendency for young people to think less for themselves and to follow media-set agendas.

Children and youth advocates lament these negative effects because they recognise the enormous, potentially positive influences media can have on young audiences-namely broadening their world outlook and destroying stereotypes, increasing communication and access to diverse ideas, and promoting critical thinking and participation in social and political life. Fueling concerns is the decline of parental supervision over young people's media habits. In part, many parents are simply too busy to be closely involved in what their children are consuming. Also, youth programming is sometimes not scheduled when most youth are actually watching, so they end up watching adult material.

In addition, it is increasingly difficult for adults to know what young people are consuming. They can't keep up with the changing television fare, electronic games and websites, and they also cannot track where their children are consuming media-in their rooms, at school, at friends' houses, in internet cafes or even just hanging out. In Japan, for example, the majority of young people possess mobile phones and more than three-quarters of them access the internet via their phone.

There is no clear consensus on what comprises quality media for children/young people. Producers, children's specialists, parents and children all have somewhat different notions, although criteria such as being credible, comprehensible and uplifting, and empowering youth to think for themselves are recognised as key ingredients. Indeed, it seems easier to agree on what quality media for young people is not: dull, boring, patronising, overly commercial or violent, vulgar, disrespectful, biased, manipulative or corruptive. While it is important to remember children and young people are as diverse in their tastes as adults, they tend to favour entertainment-oriented content, with lively and interesting characters, informal style and language, and dynamic and engaging presentation. They are also naturally drawn to subjects that interest them-music, sports, style, culture, celebrities, science and technology, etc.-and those that convey messages about how to have fun, be successful and look good.

Yet young people are not interested solely in light entertainment fare. They are also eager to learn, and drawn to information that shapes their identities, builds their sense of social belonging and makes sense of the world. They are attracted to content that entertains them, and to that which presents children and young people similar to themselves, in situations that relate to their own lives. Many young people also appreciate media content that deals credibly with topics they may find difficult to discuss with parents or adults, such as personal relationships, sexuality, AIDS, drugs, self-esteem, etc. They value factual information and advice provided by experts, as well as material prepared and presented by young people themselves.

In focus groups InterMedia has conducted in different countries, youth say they believe only young journalists can really understand their problems. Similarly, young people feel adults either miss the point or present issues in ways that are too serious, pedantic or patronising. In addition, youth in countries with widespread poverty, corruption, political turmoil and/or disease also seek realistic, relevant and meaningful content to help them understand and cope with hardships they face in their daily lives. In reality, in spite of all the media options seemingly available to many young people, young audiences aren't really given a fair choice.

There is a dearth of quality programming for youth and children across the board. There is even less choice in the majority of countries heavily dependent on foreign imports. A great deal of exported media for children and young people are produced with formats and content that can appeal to and be understood by as many cultures as possible. Thus, the prevalence of animated programming and media violence is generally driven not so much because it is what young audiences want, but largely because of competition and global marketing. Young people in the industrialised world are not all as apathetic and tuned out as they are sometimes perceived to be, and are interested in content meaningful to their lives.

Studies in Western Europe and the United States make a distinction between apathy and cynicism, i.e., young people's expression of disinterest in social and political life is often superficial and "part of the condition" of being young. For many adolescents, "cynical chic" is a way of dealing with their own sense of powerlessness and what they see as "inconsistency, complacency or hypocrisy on the part of adults." Thus, many young people will say discussion of serious issues is "boring," but they will often have interesting and informed opinions on these issues. One of the largest problems regarding media rights for youth is simply lack of coverage of children and young people in the news. What little coverage there is too often portrays youth in the context of sensationalist issues, e.g., child abuse, exploitation and violence, with little respect for the dignity and privacy of the children and scant opportunity for young people to speak for themselves.

Young people around the world feel excluded from or disserved by the media when they are portrayed simplistically as superficial, apathetic, poverty stricken or delinquent. The 2001 UNICEF-sponsored study in Buenos Aires, Montevideo and Santiago on students' perceptions of urban security issues is a good example of the media's powerful role in setting agendas and shaping opinions and images of youth. The study showed young people in these cities felt the media do not portray youth realistically or sympathetically.

Media-and television in particular-often present a negative and exaggerated picture of young people as juvenile delinquents. A majority of respondents perceived from the media that youth commit more crimes than adults, crimes of equal gravity to those of adults, and crimes at an earlier age than in previous years. This kind of inaccurate and inflammatory coverage tends to distort public and political debate in favour of repressive, rather than preventive, educational solutions to growing violence in many societies.

Dozens of examples of young people's participation in the media attest to their interest in the world around them, especially if given the chance to meaningfully express themselves on issues affecting them. A growing number of interest groups and media organizations have become involved, creating numerous opportunities for young people to participate in media. Participation takes many forms-content development, production, professional skills training and media education-and applies to television, radio, the internet, print media, video, photography and CDs. The most visible and successful youth participation programmes are usually those that incorporate the ideals of "genuine and effective" participation, i.e., an environment in which young people are involved in every step of the process from planning to evaluation.

Challenges to "genuine and effective" participation include: getting adults to let go; creating an environment at home or school where participation is serious and encouraged; overcoming cultural norms that children should be seen and not heard; and generating enough funds to sustain projects. In the last two decades, media for children and youth have become more of a global issue. Numerous players have begun to realise children's rights through the media- whether to ensure young audiences have access to diversified and high-quality media content, create opportunities for young people's voices to be heard, push for ethical coverage of children and youth, and strive for (self-) regulation of the media and for quality media education.

A broad range of governmental and non-governmental initiatives and activities speak to the growing commitment to realise children's rights through the media. Numerous meetings, conferences and summits have taken place on the subject. Excellent guidelines have been written on how to report on children's issues as well as how to ensure effective youth participation in media. Many important studies have been done exploring young people's media habits and the effects of media on youth attitudes and behaviour. Broadcasters and advertisers have adopted voluntary codes to ensure inappropriate material isn't aired during hours when young people watch or listen.

Legislation has been passed requiring television and radio stations to devote a percentage of airtime to quality children's programming. Numerous media consumer and watchdog groups hold the media to account when they do not live up to minimum standards and their social responsibilities toward the public, including children. While these are surely encouraging signs, serious obstacles to advocating for children and youth through the media remain, among them the lack of funding and political will, cultural differences, and the need for far more training for youth and for those producing material about or for young audiences. Such efforts must continue to harness the enormous positive potential of the increasingly powerful global media to make a real difference in children's lives around the world by informing them, listening to them and ultimately empowering them.

Child abuse and exploitation have figured prominently in the mainstream media in recent years, it has invariably been in the context of horrifying evidence from court proceedings, or better still, the involvement of some well-known (adult) public figure. American researchers have found that although children under 10 made up almost 20% of the US population, they represented only one in every 60 characters on primetime TV. Children's voices are not heard—especially not by the rest of the community. But then the world of television is not like the real world. Its demography reflects its purposes: to produce audiences for advertisers.

Looking at it through the prism of age reveals a population curve that, unlike the real world, but much like the curve of consumer spending, bulges in the middle years of life. That makes children and the elderly relatively neglected. This analysis of the impact of the free-market is one aspect of prevailing currents of control of media and information sources. Another is the tendency of some governments and state authorities to manipulate information, usually through tight state controls of broadcasting media, to meet political imperatives which often do not reflect the considered needs and rights of abused sections of the population.

The media industry is either a commercial undertaking which exists to produce profit, never more so than today with the growth in media outlets, achieved through new technology, bringing ruthless competition for limited markets, or it may be subject to political and state controls. In either case, journalists and media workers struggle to maintain a professional centre of gravity. In reality, it is futile for them to ignore the economic and political conditions in which they work. Yet media are, unarguably, a major influence on cultural development throughout the world; with a responsibility, many believe, particularly in sectors like public broadcasting, to inform and to educate.

The challenge facing media professionals, whether they own newspapers or broadcast media or whether they are employed to gather, edit and disseminate information, is to define rules and regulations by which they work and to articulate principles of performance which are transparent and can be tested in a public manner. But how? The question, as this paper tries to consider, requires serious examination of the way media work, of how existing principles of accountability apply, and how media must be freed from reins of political and economic control which limit professionalism and undermine ethical standards. The media's role in the evolution of commercial sexual exploitation is complex.

On the one hand, they tell the stories of abused and abuser, through news reports, photographs, documentaries, and drama. But on the other, they can themselves become the exploiter, for instance by creating sexually provocative images of children in news or advertising, or, at worst, as the vehicle for child pornography, or sources of information for paedophile networks and sexual tourism. Furthermore, the way the media portray children has a profound impact on society's attitude to children and childhood, which also affects the way adults behave.

Even the images children themselves see, especially of sex and violence, influence their expectation of their role in life. This paper does not seek to provide easy answers to complex and difficult issues nor to ethical dilemmas. But there are standards to be set and guidelines which media can adopt themselves in addressing the need for a public information policy which provides people with extensive, reliable and ethical reportage about the way children are treated in society. Although there is much that can be improved in media performance, the conclusions are not only intended to make media more accountable and journalists more responsive to systems of complaint and public scrutiny. It is also a question of encouraging debate within media about the portrayal of children and their exploitation. This is an issue which defines the good health of a just and decent society and is, therefore, a matter of profound professional concern for all who work in media.

Freedom of Expression

Journalists tend to be wary of regulators. They have much evidence to support the view that intervention in the affairs of journalism inevitably leads to forms of censorship. However, it is a legitimate question whether media self-regulation is a sufficient answer to public concern over standards of journalism in and age when the changing media landscape, and particularly the growth of global media enterprises appears, in theory at least, to put media beyond the range of national public accountability. Effective self-regulation, by which the errors of media professionals are dealt with by their peers, may not be so convincing when media organisations appear to use professional codes to support their particular interests, which in a commercial system of mass communication by no means necessarily coincide with those of journalism or the public interest.

There has been in the past criticism that self-regulation has been used to provide what might be called a iasocial alibila for the mass media industry, that is to prevent society from taking more definite (legal) measures. This argument goes to the heart of the uncomfortable balance of interests which prevails in today's media — that ethical standards are being sacrificed in defence of commercial interests. One of the principle problems lies in the implementation and enforcement of rules. Very often even regulatory bodies lack the power to enforce sanctions which bite.

In Canada in 1990, the CBC's Equity Task Force found that, with regard to equitable employment and portrayal, self-regulation and incentive measures have failed to accomplish desired and anticipated results. Some professional codes aspire to the very highest moral standards, as in Chile, Journalism and journalists must be in the service of truth, social justice, human rights and the ideals of the improvement of society and of peace among peoples. And there is no doubt that many individuals, like those quoted above, are committed to exposing and condemning sexual exploitation. Sadly, many more choose to reflect the commercial or political interests of advertisers, proprietors, or political parties. This control seldom takes the form of direct intervention or censorship, but far more often of self-censorship by the media professionals themselves—who may not even be aware that they are exercising it.

In Spain, in 1993, for example, regional and national broadcasting organisations joined with the national and regional Education Ministries in agreeing Self-regulation Principles for Television Channels concerning the specific content of their programmes with regard to protecting children and young people. The document recognises ,the significant role which television plays in Spanish society and its influence on society, particularly children and young people'. Specific guidelines on reporting child abuse could be drawn up by professional associations to accompany their general ethical codes, along the lines of guidelines for reporting AIDS published by the NUJ (UK and Ireland).

The support of media employers and regulators is crucial to improving newsroom values as highlighted by Cheryl Lai: Much of the biased or sensationalist coverage, especially headlines, is created by editors, and it will be difficult to gain improvements given Taiwan's patriarchal society unless high-level media editors and managers implement such a policy from the top down. Attitudes to censorship and freedom of expression vary widely from country to country and culture to culture. In all countries, broadcasting tends to be more highly regulated than newspapers and magazines. The importance of the right to freedom of expression cannot be under-estimated, yet it is not without boundaries.

Media in the World Today

There is increasing alarm in a number of countries that the way children are portrayed by the media today may increase the risks they face. Controversy continues internationally about how far children's behaviour is influenced by what they see on television—particularly with regard to violence. The loudest recent public controversy about the portrayal of children has focused recently on the American film Kids, directed by Larry Clark. Some critics condemned the film as voyeuristic, and expressed disbelief that the young actors, mostly amateur, who enacted the film's brutal sexual encounters, were themselves above the age of consent.

The film raised worrying questions both about the exploitation of increasingly youthful actors, and about the impact on young audiences who might regard the characters as role-models. In some countries, the film was barred to under-18s. The crucial question is whether adults themselves are encouraging children to become prematurely sexually active, or to seem to be so. This question is particularly relevant to pop music and modelling which are two of the most influential industries among young people today.

The impact of public pressure on the media should not be underestimated. Parents and educators in France, for instance, have been urged to react when TV stations show material lacking in respect for children, whether or not it is intended for young viewers. In Australia, a national campaign to improve the portrayal of women in the media included the distribution of information packs telling audiences how to complain about what they heard or saw.

For the popular music industry, international TV channels like MTV, where pop videos make up a large proportion of output, are a very significant means of reaching young people and children—even those too young to attend concerts or buy CDs. Professor Monique Remy analysed the images of young people in these videos. She found: "stereotyped masculine and feminine images, sado-masochistic scenes, Asian exoticism, fetishist female garments, women as bloodsuckers and trouble-makers, both men and women grotesquely made-up, with an element of androgeny". Women appeared as child-like, asexual yet provocative, dangerous, yet also victimised. In their analysis of 166 videos broadcast by MTV, WTBS and NBC in 1984, Barry Sherman and Joseph Dominick drew attention to the provocative style of dress, and the portrayal of young women as either aggressors or victims.

The Council of Europe's experts also warned of the ,insidious' exploitation of children's and young people's bodies in show business and the media, and the use of children's pictures or voices to create an erotic atmosphere. Certainly some media commentators have perceived this as evidence of a ,widespread phenomenon.. ..of confusion over the boundary between adults and children', in which parents have colluded in the sexual exploitation of their children. Little wonder then, the argument goes, that if the media consistently present young and old audiences alike with images of children in a sexual context, some adults will believe that children are ready and able to participate in sexual activity.

Rachel O'Brien believes it is dangerous to view these developments as ,armageddon'—a catastrophic loss of innocence about which nothing can be done. But she does perceive a widespread confusion about what childhood means, and points out that the definition of childhood itself differs from community to community, and age to age. Children are aware of their bodies, and do need to explore and learn about sex. But this should be done gradually, in a tolerant, safe environment; through natural contact with other children, and with the support of parents.

On the one hand, many children are denied sex education, while on the other there is a glorification of children in provocative poses. It seems that either we want our children to be totally innocent, or to be prostitutes. And the whole question of their rights as individuals gets left out." All this makes the notion of a ,youth oriented society' into a slogan of little substance, concludes George Gerbner. The media are oriented towards ,markets and power' rather than youth. The solution may be simple to see, but not so easy to achieve. That is, to give a voice in the media to children themselves, to listen to their views and aspirations. And to educate them to be knowledgeable and critical about how the media work.

International conventions and recommendations already emphasise the right of children to have a say in decisions affecting them, and call for a change in the way children are regarded . The Draft Declaration from this Congress also emphasises that children have a right to express their views on matters affecting their lives, and calls for children's participation in action (Article 6). Why should children not also have more say in the media? Dr

Ulla Bjornberg proposes documentary programmes on young people's lives in different countries, with the aim of giving children aged from 7 to 18—including poor and migrant children—an opportunity to air their opinions.

Children are not regarded as sources because they are not trusted to distinguish accurately between fact and fiction-a belief that also applied to children giving evidence in court until recently. New means of giving children access to the media as sources should be investigated, perhaps through the mediation of child helplines, with reassurance that information offered would be strictly confidential. Wilkinson point out that: child abuse does not fall squarely into a specific area of reporting. Is it part of the police beat, medicine, sociology, or government? The Post doesn't have a child abuse reporter per se, and I doubt that any major newspaper does. The British Home Office also decided to produce a ,good practice' video for judges and lawyers.

Governments or NGOs might consider making good practice videos for editors and journalists. Another measure to assist journalists in covering children's issues seriously and accurately would be for NGOs in each country to compile a directory of reliable experts on different topics, which could be available on every news desk. International bodies have called for more information to be given to children—both through the media and at school—about the dangers and risks of sexual exploitation, and how to defend themselves. But children, from primary school upwards, also need media literacy training, to help them understand and decode the messages they receive from both programmes and advertising, so as to become critical and well-informed media consumers.

In Canada, for instance, the organisation Mediawatch and the Federation of Women's Teachers' Associations have developed a curriculum for schools on stereotypes and gender issues. Media education can play a crucial role in counteracting the impact of these messages. Helping children to understand that media construct—as opposed to reflect—reality; that they communicate implicit and explicit values; and that they can influence the way we feel and think about ourselves and the world, are vitally important lessons. In France, an initiative aimed at implementing the UN Convention, proposes ,associating adults and children to analyse and explain the programmes on television, iethe only medium generally accessible to children of all socio-cultural backgroundsla.'

The ultimate objective is best summarised by George Gerbner again, who calls for media professionals to ,break the constraints that now bind them to markets that use but have little use for children': The need is for action towards creating a culture, and television system, that can afford to address itself to the nation's future, its children....Citizens, writers, actors and producers must work towards a system of popular storytelling whose culture-power cannot devalue and hurt children any more.

9

Newage Communication

The Internet plays a central role as an alternative, easy accessible and cheap transportation medium for all kinds of media products. It clearly shows the advantages of a worldwide and world accessible data storage unit. With respect to the sort of data stored, no restrictions apply. "Sliced-up" television is obviously an excellent option. While the Internet still offers most of its information for free, meaning without the payment of a fixed amount of money as a condition of use, it can be expected that piece-by-piece programming will only become available at a fixed price. Technically, conditional access systems can be located at the user as well as at the server end.

For both alternatives, solutions are available on the market. As for TV distribution, the first alternative continues to be more commonly used. One reason for this is that TV is still perceived as a "push"-medium and conditional access still means that the individual user can access a stream of data floating by. Another reason is that today, single feature requests are served almost exclusively over the cable network. This tree-structured network has only limited upstream transportation capability. In most cases, the customer has to place a request over a second network, in most cases the telephone network. This is called a "hybrid solution".

On the Net, most conditional access systems are located on the server side of the connection. Technically, this is the easier solution. Due to the Internet's inherently bidirectional structure, the accessing user can proceed directly from the log-in / access sites to the desired content or he or she can start to download it. As regard to the question of security, problems have been solved by the universal availability of free and standardised encryption software. Consequently, the users can locally decrypt the content they download without being dependent on any special software supplied by the server. The existence of practicable systems of conditional access facilitates the piece-by-piece distribution of movies, documentaries, and other programming on demand no matter what transportation medium is being used.

The international marketing of media products becomes increasingly attractive in a world where distances do not matter anymore. Even Germany is beyond the stage where foreign newspapers were only available in station bookstores. Cable networks increasingly transmit foreign language programming, movie theaters increasingly show films with their original soundtracks. With CNN and BSkyB, for the first time truly worldwide television channels are in existence. With increasing mobility, with better knowledge of foreign languages and with increasingly international information habits, direct marketing becomes feasible for content producers.

The Internet and satellite technologies offer excellent possibilities for them to cut intermediaries out of the distribution chain. The only way to market larger amounts of content directly and to tap into the hidden revenue sources that become visible is through on-demand distribution.

An even greater incentive for direct distribution of single media products is the prospect of creating rivalry in the use of audiovisual media content. The whole market segment of electronic information distribution is characterised by low marginal costs meaning the costs to supply an additional customer with the same content. As opposed to that, profit margins are extremely high if each additional customer can be charged the full price, as for example when selling a movie ticket. So far, this has never been possible in broadcasting. Larger audiences can only vaguely be transformed into higher advertising revenues. The consequence of this pricing model is that even high-class TV events, like the "superbowl" only generate a revenue of below $.5per viewer per hour.

Even if the costs of specific expensive programmes can not be covered entirely by the "issuing of tickets", their supply can be financed by additional advertising that can be sold more expensively due to the presence of a highly segmented audience. The economic potential created by this new form of distribution which was made possible by new technologies and by the Internet as a usage model will not remain unused.

Instead of endorsing the passive user habits of a TV viewer, convergent media like the Internet and the "customised channel" require active decisions on selection. The viewer gets bargaining power with regard to every single piece of programming that he selects because he has to pay for it separately. He gains freedom and responsibility with respect to the compilation of his personal TV programme. Broadcasting that is "sliced-up" in this way, possesses an even lower function as a "factor" of public opinion formation than an average daily newspaper which is at least composed as a combined product under editorial rules and biases.

Piece-by-piece distribution of broadcast programming lacks this very criterion of broadcasting in a constitutional sense. Through its content itself, this means of distribution will contribute to the market place of ideas in a way comparable to the press or the Internet. But the regulation regime of these media has—neither in Germany nor in the US—been characterised by a "positive order", but by an attempt to secure openness and competition. National broadcasting to a much lesser extent than some years ago fulfils its integrative function on a national level, let alone on a state level, which would be congruent with the states' legislative power in the area of broadcasting.

The driving force of the technological development that is currently witnessed in electronic media is the ease with which distances can be overcome and borders crossed. It has to be taken into account, though, that the capacity of local and regional coverage are not at all diminished but rather improved by the new technologies. Start-up companies in Silicon Valley and local heritage groups in Bavaria benefit equally from the opportunities to offer new services on new channels to new audiences. Both can take profit from the same technology. One consequence of the considerations mentioned above and the developments already underway, is the "customised channel".

The media world of the "customised channel" poses much less of a threat to the elements of the freedom of opinion formation identified by the Bundesverfassungsgericht as protected by Art. 5 I 2 GG than today's multichannel television. In particular, the "prohibition to surrender the means of the media to one group in society" and the guaranteed supply of non-mass-attractive programming are easier to achieve here than in a world of an exploding number of commercial channels. On-demand television is not only characterised by more international players but also by lower entry barriers due to the availability of alternative distribution avenues.

Herein lies the opportunity for the market for audiovisual content to reach a degree of diversification comparable to the press. The press market and its less restrictive legislation regime enacted to secure the openness of entry and coverage, has been deemed appropriate by the Bundesverfassungsgericht in order to fulfil the duties of the mass medium "press" in the process of free opinion formation. But this opportunity can only be used if the legal treatment of the new services follows the factual changes, i.e. if the individualised broadcasting services are released quickly from the structure of "positive order".

The organisational, procedural requirements as well as the content restrictions that the Bundesverfassungsgericht imposes on broadcasters actually impede new entry for small players and promote concentration of the industry. The German broadcasting doctrine is in fact responsible for a major part of the costs of broadcasting that is used to justify this doctrine. Concentration in the media is extensively criticised in Germany. But this concentration is clearly facilitated by the absence of an open competitive market for audiovisual products. In an open market, the joint control over content production and distribution is not the most effective company strategy.

Instead, an open market forces companies to focus more closely on their core areas of competence, a process which can in itself promote the development of a functioning market that creates diversity and variety. The Bundesverfassungsgericht kept emphasising the danger to content diversity that results from the assumption that commercial television will only serve the needs of mass audiences and will neglect niche topics because those productions are not commercially marketable. This might be true in an environment where competing full service programmers depend on mass audiences in order to be able to keep advertising revenues high. But such a calculation is already flawed in multichannel television because the decline in shares in the market for eyeballs is inevitable.

Broadcasters are not able to reduce advertising prices to an extent that allows advertisers to reach the same audience as in a 4- or 5-channel environment with the same amount of money. Accordingly, advertisers cannot afford synchronous advertising on all channels in order to reach audiences as in the early 1980s. This simple rationale has encouraged the number of US non-advertising channels to rise as the overall number of channels exploded. On the other hand, the dependence of powerful consumer goods manufacturers on mass audiences continues to prevent the development of an optimal diversity of programming. In on-demand television mass attraction is not a necessary vehicle for advertisement.

Moreover, it is not only possible there to further segment audiences through the creation of more niche and single interest offerings, but also to separate advertisement from programme content. Two individuals requesting the same programming can get different commercial messages. Advertising will also change in character. By more accurate targeting, informational advertising will dominate over mere "eye-catchers", because the audience is already interested in the product and does not have to be "seduced" first. Because of the new possibilities of interactivity, advertisers will not primarily try to persuade customers or to create a certain image but to "close" and consummate a deal.

Eventually, the customer will be able to control which advertising he or she wants to receive. Some advertisers will pay for the single consumers' attention through discounts, vouchers, or bonuses. The sufficient representation of national or regional content in an internationalised media world is not just a political claim, but has also entered the jurisprudence of the Bundesverfassungsgericht. The principle of "basic supply" is largely grounded on the rationale that the public-law broadcasters have to supply the audience with local, German or European content.

The "customised channel" will urge Hollywood producers to focus less on American culture but more on "western" or "atlantic" traditions in order to be able to market their products directly to a worldwide audience. When the German broadcasting concept of mandated diversity and full service 24-hour programming will be replaced by individual on-demand purchase of single products, the regulatory state will be faced with a different situation.

If in theory everybody (and in practice an unprecedented number of individuals) could become broadcasters, the footprint of the freedom of broadcasting guarantee would broaden tremendously. In this situation, governments would no longer be allowed to shape—under the justification of diversity—the basic right of Art. 5 I 2 GG in a way that only public interest institutions financed by a user flat rate fee or deep-pocketed companies can use it. Instead, governments will have to positively secure access of as many speakers as possible to the distribution media, so that the potential of the new technologies can be fully realised in favour of the goals of the diversity of opinions that Art. 5 I 2 GG wants to reach. Consequently, the German government should not have permitted the privatisation of Deutsche Telekom AG without substantial guarantees that the broadband cable network would be rapidly enlarged and upgraded.

Instead, the government should have kept the option to order a "spin-off" of the cable network branch in order to be able to invite private capital into this venture. Furthermore, terrestrial frequencies should be made available to promote wireless competition in the so-called "natural monopoly" cable. The media ownership provisions in the new media concentration law permit a market share of 3% for single owners. This might prove to be too high. The model provision for this rule, the US Telecommunications Act of 1996, deals with a country in which geographical circumstances require much larger companies and where barriers to entry in alternative media are even lower.

Theoretically, there are two ways, each of which provokes different consequences. On the one hand, one could attempt to include the new forms of media distribution into the constitutional term of broadcasting. In favour of this approach, the argument could be made that also single films, news reports, and shows and not only the whole programme of a station has a media-specific influence on the process of opinion formation. On-Demand-TV, like broadcasting streamed over the Internet, would be "broadcasting" and thus—by constitutional mandate—subject to the "positive order" regulations of licensing, surveillance, organisation and content.

On the other hand, on-demand content could be separated from traditional broadcasting. Even if the content of single features, one could argue, is the same, this form of distribution lacks the typical editorial oversight, the composition of an overall programming that is typical for the power of broadcasting among other media. Following this line of argument, it has to be decided, if these services that are no longer embraced by the broadcasting definition should become part of a new category in-between individual and mass communication with its own regulatory principles or if they should fall directly into the regime of individual communications governed by the general contract, corporations, and competition law. The individualisation of the consumption of media products that were formerly distributed as broadcasting is presently taking place.

Technological changes and economic incentives make it more than probable that in a few years the "customised channel" will be reality. Content that is individually requested from on-line data storage facilities should be treated like individually distributed print products (books) or individually requested content from off-line data storage facilities (videocassettes). Securing openness is here and there sufficient to guarantee an open market place of ideas. The new services have outgrown the confines of their former regime without threatening its objectives and can therefore be released from it without damage. Offering on-demand informational content bears none of the risks, the Bundesverfassungsgericht mentions as justifications for the special treatment of broadcasting under Art. 5 I 2 GG.

It can—on the contrary—be expected that such services will be cheaper and will be able to use many times the number of transmission facilities formerly available, including license-free transmission lines. Both aspects promote diversity and a well-balanced spectrum of opinions, which are elements of the world Art. 5 I 2 GG wants to realise. Both aspects lower entry barriers for small, local "senders" and prevent by themselves the "surrender" of the audiovisual market to one or a few groups in society. The positioning of on-demand services outside the broadcast realm is also compatible with the Court's statement that public-law broadcasting has to be able to adapt if new services take over "functions of classical broadcasting".

Thereby the Court does not subject the new services to the broadcast regime, but merely allows the public-law broadcasters to conduct business in a field ancillary to broadcasting. This is more than justified because it can be said—citing the Court's test for ancillary business by public-law broadcasters—that "especially by them the function of broadcasting as a medium and a factor in the process of free opinion formation is furthered". Currently, the two German public-law broadcasters ARD and ZDF have voluminous Internet presence.

Mass Media in the Development Process

The issue of a new international information order is bound up with ideas about the role of communication in the development of societies, on the one hand, and the relations between developed and developing countries, on the other. The purpose of development is to improve the living conditions of the members of a society. Development is at once a process and a goal. What is needed to bring about development, and what constitutes "better living conditions" have been bones of contention ever since the days surrounding national independence from the colonial powers, starting in the late 1950s, and continuing into the 1970s.

National development arose as an issue in the wake of the second world war, and the issue made its entry onto the international agenda in the 1950s. It was introduced by the USA, now a world power and interested in exporting its model of society. The Marshall Plan (economic and technical assistance for the reconstruction of Europe), and the Truman Doctrine (mutual defence against aggression by third parties) played key roles in this regard. In addition, there was the founding of the United Nations and its specialised agencies, among them

UNESCO, the United Nations Economic, Social and Cultural Organisation.

Initially, 'development' was mainly a question of economic growth, i.e., a steady and lasting increase in productivity and per capita income. There was an unshaken faith in technology and 'know-how'. Two different schools of thought developed. The more dominant of the two envisioned "the passing of traditional society", in favour of a modern, Western-style nation-state. Gradually, 'development' came to include political, social and cultural spheres, as well. The other school took its starting point in the model of socialist societies in Eastern Europe, China and Cuba and aimed, with assistance from the Soviet Union, to create nation-states with planned economies.

Here, the motor force was not the market, but political decision-making. These models of development coincided with the emergence of nationalist movements in many colonies in Asia and Africa. Modernism was part of the legacy of the colonial metropole, and the idea of a nationstate met strong and widespread resistance. At independence, however, European models of the nation-state prevailed. The new countries were in great need of assistance to combat poverty, illiteracy and unemployment.

Concepts of development were therefore paramount in politics and the economic sphere. Thus, the world of the 1960s was polarised along two dimensions: capitalism vs communism, and developed vs underdeveloped. These two dichotomies produce four worlds, but the third and fourth of these worlds, i.e., the underdeveloped countries adhering to capitalist and communist/socialist ideologies, respectively, melded and came to be referred to as the 'third world'. Their shared history and social and economic situation were more dominant than any differences that may have arisen after independence.

The countries of the third world were all characterised by low degrees of industrialisation, low per capita income, high rates of infant mortality, poor standard of public health, illiteracy, and extreme inequality. The development process became a prime focus in the contest to win the third world countries over. The role of mass media also assumed prominence in this process, not least due to technological advances. Where the modernisation school saw the problems of developing countries as the result of characteristics inherent in the history of the territories, the dependence paradigm pointed to underdevelopment as the result of capitalism and its expressions, colonialism and imperialism.

The concepts of 'development' and 'communication' are both partly normative; they stand for desirable forms of social change. As a consequence the modernisation and dependence paradigms are normative. In the modernisation paradigm, communication is seen to facilitate or hasten progress toward a modern, as opposed to traditional, society. In the dependence paradigm, it is rather a question of media imperialism. The modernisation paradigm is essentially optimistic, whereas the dependence paradigm is essentially pessimistic about development in the countries of the third world. But the two paradigms also express ideological standpoints, if by ideology we mean a system of ideas, political-economic, about the nature of the world, what it should be, and how best to go about achieving the goal.

The modernisation paradigm was dominant in the 1950s and 1960s, and the views that characterise that paradigm largely coincide with the approach to development, with a decided emphasis on development assistance, that was embraced by the UN and UNESCO at that time. But when exponents of the dependence paradigm, who were critical of the modernisation approach, demanded a change in policy in the 1960s, it marked the start of a 'war of ideas' in the international arena.

In fora like the UN and UNESCO, each national representative had access to the floor and could air his views. It was here that the non-aligned states formed an alliance to demand a new international information order. Thus, it was these two competing paradigms of development and their ideological components that constituted the fundaments for the ideas expressed in the debate on a new international information and communication that took place on the international plane, namely, in UNESCO. The concept of "free flow of information" was formulated in the USA in the final throes of the second world war. No national frontiers should be allowed to hinder the flow of information between countries.

Before the war, Europe and the USA had shared control over the international news market. The USA was, however, excluded from the extensive territories under the control of colonial powers Great Britain and France, who controlled the flows of information in their colonies. Even while the war was still raging, it was apparent that the USA would emerge from it as a world power. The U.S. saw before them a world without colonial ties, a world that lay open for an expansive economy in the U.S. The information sector was a key factor in paving the way for economic expansion.

People everywhere were tired of the propaganda and censorship that were part of the war effort and welcomed the thought of 'free flows' warmly. The idea of a 'free flow of information' was spread over the world. Newspaper publishers in the U.S. and representatives of the news agencies Associated Press (AP) and United Press (UP) travelled around the world, preaching the gospel of 'free flow'. It was particularly important to win support for the concept in the United Nations and especially its specialised agency, UNESCO. Thus, UNESCO came to be the main arena in which information and communication issues were debated in the postwar period.

UNESCO is often associated with development assistance, and in its first years the organisation was indeed primarily an aid organ. There was a great need for reconstruction within UNESCO's sphere of activity after the war, and UNESCO did what it could to muster expertise and funding for the reconstruction effort. The emphasis on material assistance was reinforced when colonies began to free themselves from colonial metropoles and became nations in their own right. UNESCO, like the UN as a whole, came to be regarded as a system for the transfer of resources from rich countries to poor countries.

The assistance UNESCO provided in the 1950s and 1960s was guided to a large extent by the faith American researchers had in the positive role mass media played in the development process, not least in promoting literacy. UNESCO assistance mainly focused on technology transfer, both hardware and software (radio and TV programmes). It was UNESCO's goal to ensure that every country had at least 10 copies of a daily newspaper, 5 radio receivers, 2 television sets and 2 cinema seats per thousand inhabitants. A second major role for UNESCO was fact-finding. UNESCO collaborates with numerous organisations and arranges meetings and conferences on a variety of subjects. These result in books and reports. UNESCO is one of the largest publishing houses in the world.

Innumerable reports the field of mass communications have been issued, with a marked peak in the late 1970s and early 1980s. The volumes report research findings, current thinking and opinion pieces, conference proceedings, and statistical compendia. This role doubtless contributed to UNESCO's becoming the principal arena of debate concerning systems of information and communication between nations and regions of the world. Finally, UNESCO also has a norm-setting function that is founded in international law. Like many other bodies within the United Nations organisation, UNESCO drafts and adopts international agreements between member nations.

Whereas neither UNESCO nor any other UN body is invested with legislative powers, they have been instrumental in bringing about numerous international agreements. Today, the UN institutions have acquired such stature that they tend more and more to be considered legal entities. The UN Charter contains clauses that require member nations to observe the Charter's legal force and to adapt national legislation accordingly (Article 104). Thus, procedures for building up a body of law have been elaborated within the UN system. A certain interplay between the UN General Assembly and, for example, the UNESCO General Conference may be observed. Issues are discussed within UNESCO and are then forwarded to the mother organisation and the General Assembly.

Flows in the opposite direction also occur. Some documents in international law have binding force for the signatories, and each must adopt and ratify the agreement individually. Most such documents are either treaties or conventions. UNESCO and similar institutions are highly instrumental in bringing such documents into the world. The Charters of the United Nations and UNESCO are, for that matter, examples of such treaties. Declarations and resolutions lack the binding force of a treaty. Nonetheless, they are of juridical significance, playing a major role in the development of international law in, for example, the preliminary work on treaties and conventions.

Declarations have higher rank than resolutions, and declarations and resolutions adopted by the UN General Assembly rank higher than declarations and resolutions adopted by specialised agencies like UNESCO. The term 'declaration' applies to documents, the purpose of which is to establish legal principles; in formal respects a declaration is similar to a convention. A resolution sets out policy for the organisation that adopts it. A resolution may subsequently evolve into a document of international law. Researchers are agreed, however, that both resolutions and declarations adopted by the UN. General Assembly must be taken into account when determining whether a given principle of international relations is to be considered part of the body of international law.

From the start, both the UN and UNESCO have had an explicit commitment to norm-setting in the field of information and communication. The statutes of both organisations contain injunctions to act to protect and promote freedom of expression and freedom of information. The non-aligned countries tabled their demand for a new international information order in the mid-1970s as an extension of already voiced demands for a new world economic order. Although the non-aligned countries could hardly be considered a unit in terms of ideology or political-economic systems and as a group had leanings toward both of the major blocs.

The geopolitical changes that took place in the 1950s and 1960s when many former colonies attained their independence led to the emergence of a third force alongside the capitalist ('first world') and socialist ('second world') blocs. The concept of a 'third world' was coined in 1955 at the milestone Bandung Conference (Indonesia) of some thirty Asian and African states. The conference adopted several resolutions of historical significance: on the abolition of colonial rule, on the realisation of democratic self-determination, on disarmament, and on economic and cultural cooperation.

What the non-aligned countries meant by a 'new international information order' can be extracted from the documentation of the movement's meetings from the period between 1973-1980. The documents from the meetings that concern information and communication have the character of political 'position statements'; they resemble statements of foreign policy and doctrine that we find in the field of international politics. They are generalised, declare a definite point of view or posture in relation to the issue at hand, and an explicit world-view.

At the same time, the statements form a sort of bridge between ideology and concrete action. It is sometimes difficult to discern specific policy objectives, guiding principles concerning how to go about realising those objectives, or proposed solutions. What we have to work with are discussions of the role of mass media and information in the development process, national media structures and media policies versus international media structures and international regulations/ policies, which touch on regional aspects and flows of media products as well as the third-world countries' relations with the industrialised part of the world.

The non-aligned countries discussed issues relating to mass media for the first time at their conference in Algiers in 1973, i.e., some years before they formulated and raised their demand for a new international information order. That the demand for reform of the world communications system arose out of the non-aligned camp was hardly sheer chance. A prime factor was the tumultuous change that was taking place in the world oil market. Oil flowed primarily from the third world to the industrial world, and the prosperity of the industrialised world depended heavily on the third world. Still, companies based in the USA, Great Britain and The Netherlands controlled the world oil market. All this changed when the third-world countries whose oil reserves were exploited began to act in concert.

Media and Modern Information Technology Globalisation

Mass media play a decisive part in what we call the globalisation process. Without the media and modern information technology globalisation as we know it today would not be possible. Access to various media, to telephony and digital services are often held forth as crucial to our political, economic and cultural development. Free and independent media are also vital to the survival and development of democracy. Meanwhile, a good share of the people of the world lack electricity and access to telecommunications and are thereby condemned to marginalisation. The development of innovative information technologies and the ongoing processes of deregulation and concentration of ownership have spurred the pace of globalisation.

Particularly communications satellites and digitalisation—not least the Internet—have had an enormous impact. These innovations have opened worldwide markets for media products such as television programmes, films, news, games and advertising. They have been a sine qua non for the formation and proper functioning of global enterprises and flows of information across national frontiers. The production and distribution of media products are highly concentrated branches, with respect to both content and ownership.

Meanwhile, traditional distinctions, between information and entertainment, between hardware and software, between product and distribution, are blurring. Much of what could be only vaguely discerned on the horizon back in the 1970s is now upon us in full force. The relationships between the rich countries and the poor countries of the world that the MacBride Commission described at the end of the 1970s seem to prevail, essentially unchanged. Issues relating to mass media have been marginalised within UNESCO, and the world today is far too fragmented for an issue like 'the right to communicate' to gain acceptance. In sum, there is no basis in reality for a political discussion of how to regulate the international media system, as was done in the 1970s.

Communication and Print Media

With the advent of the web and internet, the future has arrived. The dream of an interconnected planet where physical labour becomes minimally important and knowledge creation becomes the source of value and wealth appears to be here. For cyber-enthusiasts, the new information and communication technologies increase our choices. Digital technology can be a natural force drawing people into greater world harmony." Douglas Rushkoff believes that computers are creating a generation gap between the "screenagers" and others, with screenagers having the most important skill of all-multi-tasking, choosing and doing many things at the same time (of course, forgetting that women have always had to do many things at the same time-taking care of the home and children as well as other types of formal and informal work).

In any case, ICTs are creating a new world, an interactive, truly democratic world. For proponents, the new technologies reduce the power of Big business and

Big State, creating a vast frontier for creative individuals to explore. "Cyberspace has the potential to be egalitarian, to bring everyone into a network arrangement. It has the capacity to create community; to provide untold opportunities for communication, exchange and keeping in touch." Cybertechnologies will allow more interaction creating a global ecumene. They create wealth, indeed, a jump in wealth.

The new technologies promise a transformational society where the future is always beckoning, a new discovery is yearly. Critics, however, argue it is not a communicative world that will transpire but a world of selves downloading their emotional confusion onto each other. Far from creating a community based on consensus, the information technologies could easily create states of alienated and atomised individuals, glued to their computer terminal, terrorising and being terrorised by all those whose values conflict with their own.

Women and Global Communication

Before crying for our lost battle, we (women, non-English speaking people, not so technically-oriented individuals) can start thinking in terms of what exactly is silenced, and what can we do about it. How can we engage in global conversations while not losing our own identities, our own understanding of reality, our ways of speaking, or our own language? How can we use the Net without being used by it? Women and others do not necessarily have to be disempowered. Women have proved they can speak the language of their "enemy" (as has the South of the North). After all, that is what women learn in schools, gather from books and from all the other print media: someone else's history, someone else's perspective and someone else's knowledge.

Most feminists agree that in order to achieve this women had to either became bilingual (some successfully and many through the destructive process of othering their own selves) or to abandon their own traditional language. While it is not so clear what this traditional language might be, obvious differences between women's and men's ways of speaking are found to exist. Research, in general, shows that women ask questions while men make statements, that women talk about people and feelings while men talk about things, that women use more adjectives, more modal forms such as "perhaps", "sort of", "maybe", and more tag questions and attention beginners.

It is often stressed that language not only reflects but also perpetuates and contributes to gender inequality, and that through language hierarchy between genders is "routinely established and maintained". Feminist researchers find that men are more likely than women to control conversation while women do "support work" being some sort of "co-operative conversationalists" who express frequent concern for other participants in talk. The main solution for the transformation of current conversational division of labour between sexes cannot be only in the area of language because even the most "neutral" terms can always be appropriated by the dominant culture (like the meaning of the word "no" can be at time constructed to mean "maybe" or "wait a while").

The organisation of words and ideas into knowledge was similarly done in a context of masculine power where women were made invisible, their existence either denied or distorted and their ways of knowing and issues of interest labelled irrelevant. While many feminist linguists are attempting to reinvent language and support women's emancipation through linguistic interventions, it is clear that this has to be done simultaneously with political, economic and cultural transformations in the areas of knowledge, language and the written word.

In a future controlled by women, oral tradition, body language, sounds, dreams, intuitive and psychic ways of communicating possibly would be equal with the written text, or at least not so much suppressed. Maybe, in such a society where women would participate at all levels and in all spheres it wouldn't be necessary to introduce "dressing Barbie" video games in order to make girls more interested in new computer technologies. Maybe new software would be more interactive and more user (women/other) friendly and maybe new communication technologies would look completely different.

Maybe they would not be so individualised, and maybe, netweaving would be done in a context of community or friendly groups and not in a context of alienated individuals. Priorities would certainly be somewhere else: where the quality of life of majority of people would have the highest value. Thus, there are, and can be even more so, progressive dimensions to the new technologies. As Fatma Aloo of the Tanzanian Media Women's Association argues, "They are a necessary evil." Women and other marginalised groups must use and design them for their own empowerment or they will be further left out and behind. Without being part of the design (the "knowledge ware") and use process, they will further have to other themselves when they use the ICTs. What is needed then is the creation of a progressive information society.

It would be a world system that was diverse in how it viewed knowledge, appreciating the different ways gender and civilisation order the real. It would not just be technical but emotional and spiritual as well and ultimately one that used knowledge to create better human conditions, to reduce dukha (suffering) and realise moksa (spiritual liberation from the bonds of action and reaction). Certainly, even though the web is less rigid than a library, it is not the liberating information technology some assume-spiritual energies and shamanistic dissenting spaces cannot enter. Of course, underlying an alternative view of an information society is a commitment to prama or a dynamic equilibrium wherein internal/external, "male/female" and spiritual/material are balanced.

We need to imagine and help create social spaces so the new technologies participate in and allow for the coming of a real global civilisation, a prama, a gaia of cultures; one where there is deep multi-culturalism; where not just political representation and economic wealth are enhanced but the basis of civilisation: the epistemologies of varied cultures, women and men, how they see self and other, flourish. To begin to realise this, we need to first critically examine the politics of information. We need to ask if the information we receive is true; if it is important, what its implications are, and the who is sending us the information.

We also need to determine if we can engage in a conversation with the information sent-to question it, reveal its cultural/gendered context, to discern if the information allows for dialogue, for communication. We thus need to search for ways to transform information to communication (going far beyond the "interactivity" the web promises us), creating not a knowledge economy (which silences differences of wealth) but a communicative economy (where differences are explored, some unveiled, others left to be). To do so, in addition to engaging critically with the assumptions beyond the information discourse, we also need to expand the limited rationalist discourse in which "information" resides.

As important as cyberspace is microvita space or the noosphere being created through our world imaginations, through our increasingly shared collective consciousness. Certainly while the reality of the information era is one of exclusion, the potential for shared communication futures remains. To do so will require far more communication-sharing of meaning-than we have ever known and at far greater levels, in light of the many ways we know and learn from each other.

While we have highlighted the structures of power that create colonisation, we also need to acknowledge personal agency; we particularly need to be far more sensitive to how we project our individual and civilisational dark sides on others. The information era will further magnify our assumptions of self-innocence and other-as-guilty unless we begin to reveal our complicitness in soliloquy posing as conversation. If information can be transformed to communication, the web then can perhaps participate in the historical decolonisation process giving power to communities and individuals in the overall context of global human, economic, environmental and culturally negotiated universals.

Bibliography

Dizard, Jr. Wilson, (2000) *Old Media / New Media: Mass Communication in the Information Age,* New York: Longman.

Fidler, Roger, (1997) *Mediamorphosis: Understanding New Media,* Thousand Oaks, CA: Pine Forge Press.

Flew, T., (2002) *New Media: An Introduction,* Victoria: Oxford University Press.

Froomkin, D., (2004) "Ideas for Online Publications: Lessons From Blogs, Other Signposts," *Online Journalism Review.*

Fuller, Jack, (1996) *News Values: Ideas for an Information Age,* Chicago: University of Chicago Press.

Garrison, B., (1998) *Computer Assisted Reporting,* 2nd Edition, United States of America: Lawerence Erlbaum Associated, Publishers.

Garrison, Bruce, (1998) *Computer-Assisted Reporting,* 2nd ed. Hillsdale, NJ: Lawrence Erlbaum.

Gillmor, Dan, (2004) *We the Media: Grassroots Journalism by the People, for the People,* Sebastopol, CA: O'Reilly Media.

Griffiths, R., (1998) *Videojournalism,* Oxford: Reef Educational and Professional Publishing.

Pike, Jayna, (1991) *An Introduction to Computer Graphics Concepts: From Pixels to Pictures,* Reading: Addison-Wesley Pub. Co.

Reaves, S., (1989) Ethics: Report airs editors' debate on principles of pixels, *The Electronic Times,* Section 2, p. 1,.

Ritchlin, Fred, (1990) *In Our Own Image: the Coming Revolution in Photography,* New York: Aperture.

Rothstein, Arthur, (1965) *Photojournalism,* New York: American Photographic Book Publishing.

Russ, John C., (1995) *The image processing handbook,* 2d ed. Boca Raton, Fla., CRC Press, .

Smith, Bill, (2001) *Designing a Photograph,* New York: Amphoto Books.

Stephens, Mitchell, (1998) *The Rise of the Image the Fall of the Word,* New York: Oxford University Press.

Stroebel, Leslie, Todd, Hollis & Zakia, Richard, (1980), *Visual Concepts for Photographers,* New York: Focal Press Inc.

Szarkowski, John, (1980) *The Photographer's Eye, New York: The Museum of Modern Art.*

Index